What readers are saying

"*Hear His Voice* - how can I review this book? My heart flows through its pages and I find myself saying, "You and I, Nancy." This passion we feel, day and night it never leaves us, always there, always breathing its own breath through us. God! One with the One. There is no other reality, no other way, no other life. You have shaped your passion in this special book, your own encounter with the God of Your Being that continues to live and breathe in you. And I have shared my passion in the research I have done, pressed on by that Voice, God, the Voice that spoke to me in my third near-death experience. You flower more than I in the music of your words, still, it's the same Source, the same Love, the same Joy. I congratulate you! You completed this book, a gift to the One who gifted you, a gift to all who may touch it, read it, and be moved by it. It's God. And I rejoice with you in the power of that knowing. We share that, you and I, that moment in God's Presence. That moment that defined all our other moments. Bless you, dear sister soul, for inviting God to speak through you so that others might awaken and remember what is already written in their hearts."

—P.M.H. Atwater, L.H.D., Ph.D (Hon.);
author of *Coming Back to Life; Beyond the Light; Future Memory; The Complete Idiot's Guide to Near-Death Experiences; The New Children and Near-Death Experiences*

"*Hear His Voice* is an ecstatic, inspiring account. It shows that mysticism - that universal encounter with the Divine is alive in our modern world."

—Larry Dossey, M.D.
author of *Prayer Is Good Medicine* and *Healing Words*

"Nancy Clark speaks with the gentle wisdom gained through a Divine encounter. Read and pay attention. The truth you will find in *Hear His Voice* will set you free."

—Vernon Sylvest, M.D.
author of *The End of Fear: The Path to Freedom With the Formula*

"Extremely revealing and honest, *Hear His Voice* is written with gentleness that touches the root of the human spirit and assures us that the miracle and mystery of our true spiritual nature is authentic."

—Rodney Charles, best-selling author, *Every Day a Miracle Happens*

"Nancy Clark's book moved me to tears of happiness. She has a message about God's love in action, which will touch people deeply and motivate them to seek their own encounter with God. Like all who have been graced with mystical experience, she understands that we are never apart from God and never unloved by God. Her story will help others to understand that and to orient themselves to God-centered living."

—John W. White; internationally known author of 15 books, including *The Meeting of Science and Spirit; Pole Shift and A Practical Guide to Death and Dying*

"Until I read *Hear His Voice*, I was struggling with grief and a massive sense of failure and separation - that I had failed God, failed to even connect to any sense of purpose for this incarnation, and worst of all, failed in seeking Sacred Union. As I read the book a sense of peace began to arise - and joy - I can never be separated from that which I already am, and that I am loved and am love and light. Even though I have 'read' similar words before, for some reason they hadn't connected deep within my being until I 'experienced' them. *Hear His Voice* has been a divine catalyst of healing. Your choice that day of the eulogy has made a huge difference in my life, at a time I needed it the most. Thank you for having the courage to stay and share and love. With heartfelt thanks."

—Tracey Rieniets

"It is this wisdom that is conveyed so eloquently, with such love and intelligence, that is the most profound part of this magnificent book. This is presented in great detail, yet with manifest empathy and compassion. It's so beautifully written that it's possible for the reader to miss some of the main points, which are sprinkled liberally throughout the book. But even that's not a problem, because there's a concise synopsis of the main points at the end of the book. The message of unconditional love and acceptance from the Creator near the end of the book is one of this book's many highlights. What makes it even sweeter is the unmistakable conclusion that this book is a work of NON-fiction."

—William W. Hoover, M.D.

"I've read many books about near-death experiences and spirituality, and *Hear His Voice* is the best book I ever read. What makes this book outstanding is the author's sincerity, humility, and love as she takes us on a breath-taking journey into the domain of the Light. It is here where this inspired writing had its effect on my own personal spiritual journey. I am a better person for having read this wonderful book. I highly recommend Hear His Voice!"

—Jason Evans

"*Hear His Voice* is a fervently-told, spirit-filled account of the transformative effects that flow out of encounters with the Divine as well as the resulting insights into ultimate reality. Nancy Clark's account will be an illuminating book for all those interested in learning about mystical experiences that occur in our own world."

— Steven Fanning, PhD; associate professor of history, University of Illinois at Chicago; author of *Mystics of the Christian Tradition*

HEAR HIS VOICE

The Light's Message For Humanity:

Revelations From a Woman Who Came Back From
Heaven's Door Twice

NANCY N. CLARK, CT

1st WORLD PUBLISHING

Hear His Voice

The Light's Message For Humanity: Revelations From a Woman Who Came Back From Heaven's Door Twice

Nancy Clark

Copyright © Nancy Clark 2012

Published by 1stWorld Publishing
P.O. Box 2211, Fairfield, Iowa 52556
tel: 641-209-5000 • fax: 866-440-5234
web: www.1stworldpublishing.com

First Edition

LCCN: 2012943313
SoftCover ISBN: 978-1-4218-8647-3
HardCover ISBN: 978-1-4218-8648-0
eBook ISBN: 978-1-4218-8649-7

This material has been written and published for educational purposes to enhance one's wellbeing. In regard to health issues, the information is not intended as a substitute for appropriate care and advice from health professionals, nor does it equate to the assumption of medical or any other form of liability on the part of the publisher or author. The publisher and author shall have neither liability nor responsibility to any person or entity with respect to loss, damages or injury claimed to be caused directly or indirectly by any information in this book.

Scripture quotations are taken from *The Living Bible*, copyright @ 1971. Used by permission of Tyndale House Publishers, Inc., Wheaton Illinois 60189. All rights reserved. And *Good News Bible, Today's English Version*. American Bible Society, 1865 Broadway, New York, NY 10023. 1992.

This book is dedicated to God,
The true author.
I was only the pencil in His Hand.

"Each one of us does the work that the Lord
gave him to do: I planted the seed, Apolos watered the plant, but it
was God who made the plant grow.
The one who plants and the one who waters really do
not matter. It is God who matters, because He makes
The plant grow."

—1 Corinthians 3:5-7

ANGELS ALONG MY WAY

I wish to thank the following people who have helped me with this book. They have sprinkled a little stardust along my path while wrapping their arms around me with their unconditional love and gracious support.

Kenneth Ring, Ph.D., the world's finest scientific researcher to study the near-death experience phenomenon, my friend, thank you for encouraging me to lift myself above the clouds by reaching for the stars so that I could complete this book. I hold you in my heart with Sacred Love.

Vernon Sylvest, M.D., your absolute faith in me and your generous support for my calling is appreciated more than words can say. You are a friend forever, and forever has no end.

William W. Hoover, M.D. I am continually grateful that you never lose faith in me. You have been an enormous blessing to me.

Mark Lutz and Pat Stillisano, the angels who listened to the deepest part of my soul and who patiently encouraged me throughout the writing process.

Jan Jurkuta, you are the angel who has given so much of yourself to help me with my work for the Light. Thank you.

Columbus, Ohio IANDS organization, (International Association Near-Death Experiences): the keeper of my hopes and dreams who helped me soar with amazing grace.

Sue Vail, my editor who patiently worked on my manuscript, my sincere appreciation for the many hours you spent correcting my manuscript. Thank you!

Larry Dossey, M.D., Rodney Charles, John White, Vernon Sylvest M.D., Steven Fanning, Ph.D., P.M.H.Atwater; William W. Hoover, M.D. Tracey Rieniets, and Jason Evans. Without hidden agendas, you are the ones who graciously endorsed this book and who truly understand the importance of this book. Indeed, you are the ones who heard His Voice within when you decided to endorse this book. Thank you from the bottom of my heart!

The angels that constitute my precious family, I love you for being the ground under my feet when my head is in the clouds. My dear husband, now that you have returned to our true "home" with the Light of God, may you always know how blessed I was to have shared my earthly life with you, and that I shall love you for eternity. Ours was a loving relationship that was spiritually inspired with the care and love for one another in its many expressions. Thank you for that joy and happiness.

I wish to thank two special angels who have returned to our Heavenly Home: Reverend Tsuneo Miyashiro, you made a footprint on my heart when you took my hand in yours, and believed in my calling. My mother, you were always the wind beneath my wings who believed in me like no other. May our Creator's Light of Love be the wind beneath your Heavenly wings now and forever.

I want to joyously acknowledge my publisher Rodney Charles for recognizing and believing in the value of this book and for making it a reality. May your angels hold you until you see the Light.

Finally, I wish to thank our Creator for bringing me the help I needed to bring this book into physical manifestation for the Light's Glory, not mine. I pray that each angel I was sent who lovingly opened their angel wings to me along my path will be held in our Creator's Heart and blessed abundantly.

CONTENTS

FOREWORD

Fate, writes Nancy Clark in this spiritually inspired book, *has a way of bringing together those individuals destined to impact our lives. And so it does.*

In the early 1980's, I was at work on the manuscript for my book, *Heading Toward Omega*, when, out of the blue, I received a long letter from an unknown correspondent from Ohio. Not only was the content of this letter immediately relevant to what I was writing, but its timing was so perfect as to be almost uncanny. The writer, of course, had no idea I was working on a book, much less *what* I was writing about at that moment, but everything she shared with me about her own spiritual awakening was so germane to my purposes and so beautifully expressed that I felt as if a treasure had been placed at my author's door that I could only give thanks. Talk about an author's prayers being answered! I wrote with alacrity and gratitude to my correspondent to ask her whether I could make use of what she had so compellingly communicated to me about her spiritual experiences in my book, and she graciously consented.

So it was that Nancy Clark entered my life, right on cue, to help me with my work and mission, as if she herself were fate's emissary.

Significantly enough, the subject of my book was mainly the *aftereffects* of near-death experiences. But Nancy, it turned out, didn't have a near-death experience at all. Instead, she was fully conscious at the time hers occurred and was actually in the course of delivering a eulogy when she was drawn out of herself and thrust into a completely exalted transcendent state during which (timeless) time her consciousness was infused with profound spiritual revelations. However, when Nancy went on to describe the aftereffects of her particular experience, they were *identical* to those that had been reported by the near-death experiencers I drew on for my book. Thus, Nancy had, seemingly inadvertently, provided just the very sort of evidence I needed to make the argument that I was then developing in this book. Namely, that one didn't have to be near-death to have the kind of spiritual insights that are typical of near-death experiences and that, furthermore, the transformations that follow them, as Nancy's case showed me, can also occur without coming close to death. Therefore, as Nancy now rightly claims in her own book, the trigger or releaser for the experience is irrelevant. What happens to you during the experience is what matters, not what brings you into it.

As much as Nancy's own story was just what this author needed to help him make his brief, but what particularly struck me about Nancy's letter to me was her absolute conviction that she had been commissioned, as it were, by what near-death experiencers tend to call the Light (but others simply call God) to communicate what she had learned to others. Her letter, then, wasn't just meant for me alone but was at the time truly meant for me to share with a wider audience, on Nancy's behalf. She needed me, too, to serve as a channel and to broadcast to my readers what she could not then do on her own. She had the message, but I had the means to deliver it. I now believe she was guided by the Light to write her letter to me; we were meant to work together. And indeed, I quoted Nancy throughout the later portions of my book, and she was the very last experiencer I cited in my concluding summation. So much were we aligned in our understanding of the implications of these extraordinary encounters with the divine.

But if I were mainly an instrument, then it was already clear, even more than twenty years ago, that Nancy herself was destined to do more than speak through others - her own voice ultimately needed to be heard. As she wrote me at the time:

The most important goal in my life is to use my experience in a positive, meaningful way to help others. There is no doubt in my mind I will accomplish my mission on this earth. I firmly believe that this experience was given to me as a gift to be shared with others. I WILL make a meaningful contribution to the research and application of the life-after-death phenomenon, regardless of the skepticism I shall encounter from those I reach out to.

I am motivated only by the gratitude I feel in being a recipient of this experience. For giving me a glimpse for a few moments of a life beyond the present one, I owe it to my fellow man to lovingly share this great truth with them.

When I ultimately make my transition to the next world and meet Him again I'll say, "Lord, for the precious gift you gave to me while I lived on the earth, I did my very best work for you. This is MY gift in return to you.

What Nancy didn't divulge to me then, but what I later learned from her, was that the Light had directed her expressly to write a book.

This book.

A book that would tell the full story of that experience she had shared with me (and my readers) only in part - the story of her awakening into the Light and the changes that awakening had brought into her life, which have been nothing but a form of service to and for the Light ever since.

Nancy's awakening took place a quarter of a century ago - on January 29, 1979, to be exact - so this book has obviously had a long gestation. But it is the better for that because in her life of service, Nancy has by now amassed many further experiences that have deepened her insights and honed her spiritual wisdom so that this book is no mere narrative of Nancy's life but a profound distillation of the teachings of the Light, written in such a way as to help the reader become transformed just as Nancy has been. For what the Light instructed Nancy to do - to make her chief mission is - to pass on to others what was revealed to her in order that those who are touched by her words can discover the Light - and the love, the infinite love - within themselves and thus begin to live from their true selves, in God, now awake to the Real World.

Nancy has entitled her book *Hear His Voice*, but I would perhaps modify it to read Hear *Her* Voice - not to elevate Nancy herself, but to make it clear that it is her distinctive voice that speaks for Him in this book, and when she speaks for Him, her voice is inspired. You can feel the Truth in it, and when you open yourself to it, you, too, will be able to open yourself to your true nature, which is only love, and by awakening this love in yourself, to act more lovingly in the world.

It is not for me to judge, but I think by the time you finish this book, you will agree with me that Nancy has indeed fulfilled her promise to the Light she made so long ago. Through her own Light, she has made His shine more brightly. But we must also acknowledge that it is Nancy's life of service, and not just this beautiful expression of it, that is her true and enduring testament to the Light.

—Kenneth Ring, Ph.D.

Professor Emeritus, Psychology, University of Connecticut
Author, *Lessons From The Light, Heading Toward Omega*

COMMENTARY: HOW AND WHY THIS BOOK WAS WRITTEN

After I entered Heaven's Door twice, I was called to write this book as a summons from a Higher Power to be a servant of the Divine. That may sound like a grandiose statement, but I assure you that I am acting upon something greater than egotism. My mission, so to speak, is of the highest, for it gives expression to the Sacred by reminding us of the inner voice that beckons us to reconnect with the Beloved. So in a sense, this book is a calling for all of us to redefine our own sense of identity - of who we are, why we are here, and what life is all about. It is a call to cherish and love one another and all that the Creator has created - a gift to us.

This book is motivated by several extraordinary encounters with the Sacred that touched my heart and soul so deeply that I was forever transformed by the incredible power of Divine Love. You will read about the time as a very young child, I heard the voice of our Creator telling me that I was loved, and you will learn how my spiritual life instantly blossomed after that encounter with my Beloved. You will also read about my near-death experience during childbirth when once again, my Beloved appeared before me. That near-death experience prepared me years later to receive the amazing Grace of yet another much deeper, Sacred mystical or near-death-like experience that resulted in ultimate union with the Divine. That invitation granted to me by the Light of God to enter Heaven's Door a second time was manifest for a Divine Purpose. The resulting change of consciousness that experience produced, awakened me to the understanding that the Sacred is the reality of my being. The great love enfolding me during my union with the Creator was the very essence of the life-force within me, a love and joy indescribable. As a result of that profound transcendent experience, I am writing this book focusing primarily on this Sacred mystical near-death-like experience and what my Great Teacher revealed to me in order that I may share this knowledge with others.

I speak the truth, it was not my idea to write this book. The directive was placed in my mind by the Light during a mystical experience that occurred to me in 1979 that was similar to Saint Paul's conversion experience on the road to Damascus as recorded in the Bible, the revelation experience described in *"A Course in Miracles,"* and very similar to currently, what is called a near-death experience with the exception that I was not close to death at the time, suffering serious illness or physical trauma.

My experience is subjective evidence that one does not have to die first in order to transcend our physical sense reality and encounter the Divine. Simply put, it was an experience of direct communication from the Light who encompasses pure love, joy and ultimate knowledge. This experience not only transformed my life but also altered the course of my life's work.

Because of the unusual nature of encountering our loving Creator and the tremendous impact it had upon me, I learned that our unworthiness **will not lessen our Creator's love for us** and that silence should not be mistaken as a sign of the Creator's absence or abandonment. Divine love does not depend upon our religious affiliation, our good works, our desires, or our love for our Creator. Our Beloved sets **no conditions** upon this precious love for us.

Throughout the book are the direct insights of the nature and love of the Light that our Heavenly Creator inspired me to

I only wish to communicate a sense of a personal Deity, one who has a personal love and concern for **everyone**. I use the pronoun He, to convey this intimate, personal Being only as a means of communication. Imagine your own understanding of a personal Deity. There is no right or wrong way.

I consider myself to be a spiritual being whose eyes have been opened by the Grace of the Light to bring forth a loving message to humanity. Some would say that I am a mystic. In the true sense of the word, I am. However, I say with great humility that I am simply a child of the Divine nestled close to the bosom of the Light's Love and seeking only to be an instrument of that Holy Love to others. In the deepest sense, I am not the writer of this book; I am only the pencil in my Great Teacher's hand. Spirit did the inspired writing through me. How?

I learned from my mystical near-death-like experience that there is but one power that is working in and through all of us, Divine Light. As one recognizes and lives continually in the full, conscious realization of his/her oneness with the Creator, our thoughts, acts, and purposes are lifted up to a Divine standard. One's spiritual nature becomes imbued with peace and Divine Love and creates a willingness to open one's self to the inflow of that Divinity. It pours through us to the degree that we open ourselves to it. By surrendering our ego needs to a Divine purpose, we embody that purpose in ourselves and we are then able to share it lovingly, with others.

I knew it was absolutely essential for me to release all ego attachments for the manifestation of this book if I wanted to be used as an instrument for Divine Purpose. Ego is a very strong motivator in human beings. It enables us to make great strides in all areas of our human lives. It serves a very useful purpose but it has no place whatsoever in spiritual practices. I had to rid myself of my own need to dictate what I felt the reader should read. Instead, I developed a complete willingness to "let go and let the Light of God guide me."

This release allowed my spirit self to emerge which would be in harmony with Divine Purpose. Before each writing session, I listened to Kitaro's "Silk Road" and "Reimei," and soft classical music, in particular, Jules Massenet, "Meditation," performed by the Royal Philharmonic Orchestra, London. This song is a very powerful catalyst for enhancing my spiritual reverence. The exquisite flowing sound of the violin cascaded over my senses, lifting me higher and higher to the quiet awareness of the Holy Spirit within me. Kitaro's gifted music captures my soul's expression of love for our Creator in the way no words can describe. The spirited sound of the heavenly music flooded my mind and body with blissful joy and silent peace.

Like a swelling rose bud waiting the moment of birth when it would fully reveal its inner radiance, my heart was germinating the seed of love toward the One who transformed my life. I prayed that the Light would help me write this book that I was instructed by the Light to write during my mystical union with the Light. I prayed that the contents would be truthful and bring glory to our Creator. At that point, my heart was opened so wide, so high, that at times tears streamed down from my eyes because of the joy unspeakable. I felt the nearness of the Light's Presence, and it overwhelmed me. After letting go and opening up to the Light of God in prayer, I found that the writing began to emerge effortlessly. It struck me as being odd because writing does not come easily to me. Usually I write a sentence or two, stop, think about the words I am using and if I can rewrite those words in a more meaningful way. The process is painstakingly long and tedious. But while I was writing this book, I am convinced that a Higher Power was the writer and I, only the pencil in that writer's hand, because of the ease with which it was written.

After each writing session, I would return to prayer and thanked the Light for the inspired words that formed on the paper. I would stay in the stillness for a long time, rededicating myself to Divine Purpose. Often times no words were spoken.

The stillness spoke words I could not speak. The soul speaks words that language has not developed. In this sublime silence, I became pliable as putty in the waiting hands of the Divine, willing to be molded into any form Spirit desires and whenever Spirit chooses.

Rest assured that my Great Teacher has given me a directive to write this book based upon my direct encounter with the Light of God. It would be morally impossible for me to broadcast lies, deceit, and falsehood. My responsibility is only to share lovingly, the direct knowledge that I have attained as a result of my communion with the Light when I made my journey to that Ultimate Reality. The reader will choose either to believe or disbelieve. It will not be my intent to cajole, manipulate, or indoctrinate the reader's free choice. I will simply share what I have seen with my own eyes and heard with my own ears - the sacredness of that Divine Reality. That is my promise to the Light, myself, and to you. I will return "home" one day and I will stand before my Creator, and as I do, I will truthfully be able to say, "I accomplished the work you directed me to do. It was the best gift I could give you in return for the gift of Grace you gave to me."

Dear reader, I ask only one thing of you as you read this book. Read from your heart, not your head. Allow your spirit self to emerge while setting aside your ego need to question, judge, and doubt. In doing so, you will open yourself to the rich inner wisdom as you elevate your consciousness to oneness with the Divine. Let the soft, inner voice of your spirit-self awaken within you, the spiritual wisdom already given to you from Spirit. Deep within your soul lies a wellspring of knowledge awaiting the trigger for release. Faith is the key that unlocks that treasure. Spiritual understanding comes to those whose eyes are open and whose ears can hear.

—Nancy Clark

CHAPTER 1

REFLECTIONS OF A MYSTIC

*The wise man recognizes the Holy place of his own soul.
He continually seeks to expand his awareness of the Divine
Presence whose candle of Light blissfully burns within him.*

By the time you finish reading this book, I hope you will understand that human consciousness can be raised to a higher level where life and the order of the universe is indescribably hopeful. The wisdom that I am going to share with you is not based upon my own opinions or taken from any school for higher learning. The wisdom came directly from my mystical encounter with the Light and perceived in such a manner that transcended my limited awareness of the nature of our Creator and ultimate reality.

In 1979 while delivering a eulogy for a dear friend, I had a life-changing experience in which there was a metamorphosis from my external ego self to some unknown internal mechanism which I believe was my soul becoming one with the Mind of our Creator. Suddenly, in one flashing departure from the ordinary earthly sphere of existence, my consciousness lifted to a higher spiritual realm that was hidden from me previously, and in which lucidity drew aside the veil between illusion and reality. False conceptions inhibited by past fears and doubts disintegrated and were replaced with new understanding, revelations, beauty, love, Light, Light, Light!

Sometimes we face many difficult roads on our journey before we attain the full stature of a spiritual human being. I learned a very important lesson from my transcendent experience. Each one of us is purified by the darkness the mystics call the dark night of the soul, a feeling that God has deserted us. Our pain and suffering, the failures of our endeavors, the betrayals we experience are actually blessings in disguise. Those moments of crisis or darkness are actually the beginning of a deeper intimate experience of our Creator calling us to grow beyond where we are at that particular time of our spiritual growth. We may not be able to understand why bad things happen to good people, but those bad experiences do not tell the real story of a person. It is not how much a person has suffered or failed that tells the story of that individual. The real story is found in the triumphs and over comings, and in spite of the hardships, that person still persisted toward that journey toward wholeness.

As we make our passage through life, our experiences, the good and the bad, are ultimately, the growth of soul and as we draw closer to our Beloved throughout our lifetime; gradually, a transformation takes place so that we begin to take on the mind of Spirit - to see our world and the people as Spirit really sees them.

Where we come from, why are we here, where do we go when we die? This knowledge is the foundation of religion and is the foundation of the human quest. Deep within the heart of every human being lies the desire for the Divine. Our Beloved implants it in our very souls so that we can create ourselves as living and inborn beings who find their oneness with the Creator of all reality. Man is always searching for a better life, meaning, and purpose. The reason is that our soul is restless. Our soul always pushes us toward some great intent in order to reveal manifestations of our Divine attributes in accordance with Divine purpose.

Mystics throughout the ages tell us that it is important to develop soul growth in order for the growth of a whole and inwardly sound personality through whom the life force can flow. Our latent powers are within us so that we can create ourselves as living beings who are at one with the Creator of all reality. I was indeed blessed to have had such a transformative experience that created such a solid foundation of love and understanding, but I learned from my Great Teacher that everyone aids in the fruition of Spirit by the countless manifestations which we can bring to being through our gifts and through our own soul growth.

I will share my life with you in an endeavor to show you that you too, can awaken to the rights of an evolved soul and come into your Divine Inheritance, the treasure of Infinite Spirit. My life saga is revealed to show you that the insights we discover ourselves can change us deeply. Without that attention, the current of life simply passes us by, and we cannot awaken our true nature. As you read about my life, keep in mind that the sole reason for sharing it with you is to show you that the roadmap of your life's mission is composed of all your little experiences, the good and the bad. You will see that my life experiences helped to open my mind to see our Creator's wondrous plan for me, and our Creator's plan for everyone. No matter what your life experiences, eventually you will enter into a greater state of consciousness and what once had been difficult to understand becomes plain as the nose on your face.

share with others. The Light's voice can be heard in the stillness of your heart as you read and reflect upon the Light's love for **you**. Pay attention to those wondrous moments and know that the Light's voice is expressing the desire to draw near to you. **Hear His Voice!**

As a result of my Divine encounter I no longer believe that a Creator exists. **I know** our Creator exists. The Light's love for **all of us** is beyond human comprehension and because of this, the Light can find many ways to speak to us that are beyond human comprehension. You will read about some of the mysterious ways of communication that offer penetrating insights into a spiritual realm of existence that parallels our physical reality.

An aftereffect of that Sacred mystical experience is my burning desire to love and serve the Divine above all else. No, I am not a religious fanatic. If what I say corresponds to any or all religious faiths, it is only because Divine Love is universal and finds its intimate rest within each soul regardless of that individual's religious orientation. There may be many different belief systems, but within each belief system lays the underlying importance of recognizing and accepting the presence of "inner light." This spiritual consciousness transcends the physical sense reality and herein lays the universal love manifested by our Creator and made available to all of us. That is why someone living alone on an isolated island can be as close to our Creator as someone residing in the rectory of a majestic and holy cathedral.

During my encounter with our Creator, I did not experience the Creator as being either masculine or feminine, but rather, all-inclusive. Divine nature is ineffable; therefore, I wanted to convey more of the personal intimate Being I encountered in order that the concept of our Creator can be made image-able. Use any word that will allow our Creator to become real to you; visualize an image or that which inspires unity and genuine trust in the Deity. Too often, our language and personalizing the Deity results in rejection of the One who is beyond conceptualization.

CHAPTER 2

LOOKING BACK

A simple prayer of the heart is precious in the eyes of our Creator. Our Beloved who loves us gives us a Holy rest and the blessed assurance that the Holy One is there in the dazzling obscurity of our Secret Silence.

There are many ways people learn about our Creator, e.g. religious scholars, clergy, churches, synagogues, universities, books, movies, etc. I had no formal training about our Creator, but I would like to tell you how I came to *know* our Creator rather than knowing *about* our Beloved. It is my hope that as you turn each page in this book you will clearly see that our Creator has the absolute authority to open our eyes and hearts to a more profound understanding of our Beloved's Divine nature, no matter who that person is, how young, how old, how educated, how uneducated, or what religion a person had or did not have. I would like to tell you how I first met my Beloved.

My early childhood roots played an important role in preparing me to receive the gift of my Holy Heavenly encounter with the Light in my later adult years. I recall as a small child having had a wee mystical experience that activated my spiritual relationship with our Creator and set into motion the deep reverent love I felt for my Beloved for the rest of my life. I am a

Ukrainian Catholic. My grandparents fled Ukraine during the Russian Revolution and managed to settle in a coal-mining town in Hazleton, Pennsylvania. The language spoken in our home was mainly English laced with Ukrainian so that everyone could understand one another. My grandparents spoke very little English. Simple words were spoken which reflected the non-intellectual life we all led.

I was born in 1941 and times were very hard then. World War II began, and men were needed to fight the war. My father joined the navy and was sent to the Philippines as a Seabee constructing runways for our warplanes to land. While my dad was away at war, mother and we three children lived with grandma and grandpa. My childhood days were filled with laughter, love, and joyful moments spent with grandma baking bread and the best poppy seed rolls imaginable. We were poor, but I never knew it. I felt deeply loved and secure.

The earliest memory I have is of a three or four year-old little girl sitting on a church pew, her tiny legs just barely dangling over the edge of the wooden oak pew. My mother always made me sit to her left and my two brothers to her right. "Sit still, be quiet, don't turn around to look at people," mother would say. "We are in God's house now and you must be very good children."

God's house? I wondered. Who is God? What does God look like? I don't see Him, I thought. Then mother explained to me that God lives far away up in Heaven, up past the sky. The church was a place where God's Spirit lives, and it is a very Holy place where people come to visit Him. I didn't understand what God's "Spirit" was, but my mother answered my questions, and that's all I needed to know at that time.

Going to church every Sunday was BORING! We went to High Mass (the longest of the two masses - almost two hours long!) Not only did I have to sit still and not fidget for two hours, but I also couldn't understand a word the priest said. He spoke entirely in Ukrainian since the majority of the people who belonged to the church were Ukrainian immigrants. I could understand the language in our home because we spoke simple sentences; "Close the door, wipe your feet, supper is ready," and so on. The priest was speaking words I never heard in our home. His words reflected a superior degree of intellectualism about a subject that I knew nothing of.

Seated in the pew, I just stared at the priest watching his every move. I couldn't understand why a man would want to dress up in something called a "robe." It looked like a woman's long dress to me. A very long necklace hung from his neck and fell to his waist where a tasseled rope-like looking belt hugged his thick waist. Mother explained to me that the necklace he was wearing was the "symbol of the cross." Draped over his hands was something that looked like a bracelet with pretty colored beads. Once again, mother explained that it was the "rosary."

I couldn't understand anything mother was trying to teach me about this odd looking man who talked in a weird language. To confuse me more, at times this man that mother called the "priest" walked around the altar whirling a gold pot hanging from a long golden chain. Smoke was gushing out from the top of the pot. As he stood in front of the people sitting in the pews, he whirled the pot as high as his shoulders so the smoke would reach everyone. I always coughed when the smoke touched my nose, and I asked mother why he was doing this. She told me that he was "blessing everyone."

Nothing made any sense to me, and I hated coming to this place every Sunday. It was an ordeal for my brothers and me to follow the rules of etiquette which mother made us adhere. But we knew if we didn't follow them, our little behinds would get tanned when we got home. Choice was not an option. We obeyed Mother's rules. Seated like a rigid statue in the church pew, I decided that I had to do something to occupy myself during the two-hour church service. I thought, "Since this is where God lives, I'll talk to Him silently since I wasn't allowed to speak aloud."

I can still remember that day as if it were yesterday. Silently in my mind, I started talking to God explaining why I couldn't talk out loud. Wondering if God could hear my silent words, I continued to talk about my family, and the activities that I did all week. I told God about the pierogis that grandma and I made for supper Friday night and asked God if He had ever tasted them. "They're delicious," I said. "First you make a dough out of flour, water and stuff. You roll it out thin, cut them in squares, then put a spoonful of mashed potatoes on the dough and then you fold the dough over the potatoes and pinch the edges closed with your fingers." I said. "Then grandma puts the pierogis in boiling water, and I have to tell her when they float to the top. Here's the best part God, Grandma takes them out of the pot and puts them on my plate with lots of melted butter, fried onions and sour cream. I can eat a lot of pierogis God; they are delicious!" I said in quiet conversation with God in my mind.

I talked to God as if I were talking to my mother. Words kept flowing effortlessly. My eyes were open, but my intense focus on my silent conversation with God obliterated all my surroundings so that all I saw was a misty, fog-like presence before me. I no longer saw the priest, the altar, the altar boys, and the stained glass windows. Deep in a meditative-like state, I was able to transcend unknowingly, to a place where I felt so safe and loved and where I was nestled close to my friend, God.

I remember saying in my thoughts, "I have to go now God, but I love you very much. Thanks for listening to me." Then clearly and unmistakably, I heard a masculine voice in my head saying, "I love you also my child." My mother's elbow beside me disrupted my prayerful state and I soon returned to full awareness of my surroundings. It was time to leave. Mass was over.

I never told mother about my silent conversation with God that day, but from that day on, I couldn't wait to go to church on Sundays. All week I would collect and save all the thoughts I wanted to share with God during the service on Sunday. I was easily able to transcend my physical boundaries and enter that wondrous place where my friend God was, simply by praying. I never heard God's Voice again as I did that first time, but I knew our Creator was always close beside me, closer than my mother sitting next to me. I felt a loving bond with my Beloved that was **REAL** and not a figment of my young imagination.

Perhaps that is why I developed spiritually at such a young age. This was evidenced by the way I continued my relationship with my Beloved at home. For instance, immediately after church services, I would return home, take off my nice Sunday dress and head straight for my parent's bedroom and play "church." In secret, I would stay in the room and remove all the items from the top of the dresser and pretend it was a church altar. I would place my cross of Jesus in the center of the altar and beside that, a bottle of cologne became a candelabrum, and a red vase became the Holy Communion vessel. The lace doily adorning a nearby chair was used as a hat to cover the top of my head, and my father's bathrobe became a Holy robe worn by a little girl who became in her vivid imagination, a Holy priest. Carefully and methodically, I re-created the church service I had been to. This re-creation allowed me to speak English words and find my own meaning throughout the Holy service being conducted in the sparse bedroom of a row house on Cranberry Avenue. I felt close to my Beloved - very close. I felt loved by our Creator, and I loved God more than anyone or anything else. An instinctive spiritual nature had awakened within me poised and ready to grant me the joy of expressing my impassioned love for my Creator.

Grandma's house was approximately one and one-half miles from our house. My brothers and I would walk that distance frequently to visit her. Sometimes we would take the wooded route through Bendybrook, and other times we would walk up Popular Street through Saint Gabriel's Cemetery. Across the street from the cemetery was Holy Rosary Church where a beautiful outdoor grotto stood. It was a serene garden setting where one could go to pray or light a candle before the statue of the Virgin Mary. I never walked past the church without stopping by the grotto to pray and profess my love for my Beloved. My brothers always waited for me in the cemetery while I prayed in the grotto, and sometimes they would hide behind the headstones and scare me when I walked through to find them. Although my brothers told me macabre ghost stories in the cemetery, there was something to revere about Saint Gabriel's Cemetery. I always felt the need to pause at a grave and say a hushed prayer.

A few years ago, I visited my Aunt Nadine who still lived in grandma's house, and we drove past the grotto at Holy Rosary Church. "Stop the car Aunt Nadine, I want to visit the grotto," I exclaimed. We pulled into the parking lot, and she let me walk over to the grotto by myself. I kneeled down and began to pray. Warm memories of that small child inside of me surged through my consciousness, and once more I felt the child-like innocence of my love springing forth praying in the grotto before my Creator as I had done so many years before. Walking back to the car, I heard the church bells ring and felt heartfelt gratitude that the grotto was still there all these years. My roots had grown very deep in Hazleton, and the grotto was a place of Holiness where my spirituality blossomed.

April showers bring flowers in May. Oh, the joy of Spring! I waited impatiently every year for the month of May to arrive with as much excitement as a child receiving Christmas gifts in December. For the entire month of May, I erected a "May Altar" in my bedroom. In a designated area, I placed a cardboard box. In the center, I placed a beautiful stone statue of Jesus that mother bought for me from the pawnshop for this very special face as I placed it upon my May Altar. I continued this tradition until I married. My young spiritual life continued to flourish through the years. My intimate relationship with our Creator was so precious to me that I once considered becoming a nun. That idea faded however after I reached puberty and discovered the opposite sex!

My life was extremely happy. I had a family who loved me deeply. I pursued a successful modeling career, won many beauty contests, became an Arthur Murray dance instructor, and graduated from Women's Medical College at the University of Pennsylvania specializing in cytology, the study of cells.

Throughout this period in my life, my relationship with our Creator was extremely close. I always knew that my Beloved was the music within the limbs of my being, enabling me to dance to the melody of my heart and my soul. Joyous thanksgiving sprang from my heart praising my Beloved for this wonderful life that was given to me. Little did I realize up to that point that all the interactions and achievements with the external world were the desires within my heart arising from the desire of Spirit to bring me the substance of a happy, fulfilled life and that Spirit was preparing me for a much greater life later on.

CHAPTER 3

A TURNING POINT

Those who walk in darkness are further from the Light than the Light is to us.

Many years had passed since that day I spoke with our Creator in my mind as a young child in that small Ukrainian church. My life had been so richly blessed with the Holy Presence, but there came a time when devastation struck my consciousness, and I found myself separated from the center of my life - my Beloved. A major decision, which directly impacted my life, took place. I fell deeply in love with a wonderful person. He was a person whose values reflected my own, with one exception - religion. Dean was a non-Catholic.

Our deep love for one another eventually led to the inevitable, marriage. After we set the date for our wedding, we had to meet with the priest to arrange all the details. The first order of business was to have marriage counseling sessions with the priest so that as a couple, we would be well prepared to begin our marriage together. The first session was disastrous! We sat with the priest as he discussed the procedures for the wedding day. We were both excited visualizing the moment when we would be joined as husband and wife. Then, reaching in the top drawer of his desk, the priest pulled out a piece of paper and handed it to Dean to sign. "What's this?" Dean asked. The priest replied,

"It's the document that you have to sign that states both of you promise to raise any and all children that you may have as Catholic. It's our church law." "No way," declared Dean. "I won't sign this! I believe in letting the children decide for themselves what religion they want to be."

I could feel all the muscles in my body contracting and my heart beating faster and faster. Panicked thoughts flooded through my mind. Oh no, what am I going to do? Dean, just sign the paper. Do anything the priest asks. Don't rock the boat. We could let the children decide what religion they want to honor when they're old enough. Just sign - SIGN!

Dean didn't hear my silent screams. He continued talking about how he won't take away his children's right to decide what they wanted to believe in. Then, just as I dreaded, the priest turned to me and asked, "Did you know that Dean feels this way?" "Yes," I sheepishly replied. "Under these circumstances, I can marry you in my office, but not in the sanctuary, which is only for Catholics who promise to raise their children in the Catholic faith." He told us to go home and think very seriously about the matter and inform him of our decision. Then, looking sternly in my eyes he said, "And you, young lady, I want to counsel you privately in my office beginning tomorrow evening at seven o'clock." I felt like a schoolgirl in the principal's office, feeling guilty about something I had done but wasn't sure of what I was guilty. Obeying his command, I told the priest I would come the next evening.

Dean and I walked in silence to our car both of us lost in our own thoughts. Finally, Dean broke the silence and asked me what I wanted to do. I was confused, immobilized by fearful thoughts. What would we do? Dean sensed my utter dismay and tried to comfort me. "I know that must have been very hard for you, but I have to stand up for my own beliefs, just as you have to stand up for your own beliefs," he said. He was right, but it still didn't solve our problem. What would we do?

The next evening at seven o'clock, once again I was seated facing the priest as he sat authoritatively behind the massive wooden desk. Why am I here? I wondered. What did I do? I felt scared and alone. I noticed the priest's white collar pressing tightly against his throat. His face was red. I sensed this was not going to be a friendly chat. "Did you know that Dean is not Catholic?" he asked as I nervously sat in my chair. "Yes," I said quietly. Reluctantly, I started to state Dean's position on the matter, but he didn't want to discuss Dean. He wanted to talk about me. "If you knew he isn't Catholic, why didn't you influence him so that he would convert?" he asked.

What followed was a two-hour-long session with the priest challenging every excuse I offered in support of Dean's position not to convert to Catholicism. I was not gaining ground. At one point in our discussion, the priest told me, "It is your responsibility as a Catholic to convert him to Catholicism. Because you have failed to do this, you are an unworthy Catholic. God is watching over you and sees that you are not converting Dean, and God is disgusted with you." *Ouch!* He just delivered a powerful guilt trip on me! God is unhappy with me. I wanted to beg my Beloved not to be angry with me, but the priest immediately stood from his chair and started to escort me to the door. "Young lady, I want to continue these sessions with you three times a week for two hours a session." I agreed, silently hoping for resolution of this problem.

At this point, I would like to clarify something. Remember, as a child I was raised in the Ukrainian church where no English words were spoken. Thus, I had no formal intellectual knowledge of the Holy One, Jesus, or even the Bible. Back in those days, our church priest instructed us not to read the Bible because of the possibility of misinterpreting it. We were told that during every Mass the priest would read scriptures from the Bible (in Ukrainian), then he would speak a sermon (in Ukrainian of course), relating to that scripture. The priest was viewed as a very Holy figure with greater understanding of the Bible than lay people. It was almost considered a sin to read the Bible by oneself.

These events may be difficult for those of you who are not Catholic and in particular, Ukrainian Catholic in the 1940's and 1950's. Changes within the church **have taken place** since then, but I want to try to tell you what it was like at that time **for me**, so that you will understand my mind set at that time. Through the influence of my mother and grandparents who were devout Ukrainian Catholics, I trusted that they would teach me all I needed to know to be a faithful Catholic. After all, they could understand and communicate the Ukrainian language. They would simply tell me what the rules were, and I adhered to them because I believed that priests were not merely mortal men, but rather, our Creator's right hand servants on earth. They were especially handpicked by our Creator and were so holy that every word that passed their lips was a true and holy message of the Holy One. I placed them so high on a pedestal that their feet never touched the earth's surface. They were imbued with Heavenly truths and to question that authority was a sin, a grave sin! To knowingly sin against our Creator for one's own sake was absolutely the worst kind of sin one could commit. The rules are the rules, period. Do not question the rules, just follow them. That was the mid set in those days and like a little lamb, I followed.

For the next four weeks my sessions with the priest continued. His intent was to show me that I was the worst Catholic person he had seen because I was refusing to convert Dean to Catholicism. My intent was simply to show the priest that I believed *"if"* I were sinning, God would forgive me. I didn't think that I was such a bad person. Every time I tried to make my point, the priest would interrogate me with his viewpoint with cutting words like, "You are the scum of the earth. God cannot forgive your sin. God can forgive a murderer, but not you. Don't even pray to God anymore because God doesn't want to listen to you. Don't go to church anymore either because you are not worthy to step inside his clean sanctuary. You are filthy and you are not fit to be in God's presence. If you do, you will feel the wrath of God upon you."

WOW! His words pierced my very soul! At the end of the month, I was spiritually shattered. No matter how hard I tried to communicate my deep love for God and God's love for me, the priest was able to tear down my beliefs. What resulted was a loss of my own personal power and self-esteem. I took on as **truth**, the priest's perceptions, and I discarded mine. I was left, spiritually naked. There was not even room in my heart and soul for a speck of hope in a God who could love me. If God could not love me, I certainly could not love myself. I truly believed that my entire being was composed of raw sewage. I was the worst human being on the face of the earth. The priest who I believed was our Creator's emissary on earth told me I was, so **I was!**

Let me remind you of the mind set I had in those days. Priests were so holy and held dominion over me because I believed that all their words were Divinely inspired and came directly from our Creator. Since I firmly believed that our Creator judges us after death and sends us either to Heaven or to Hell, it was natural for me to accept the fact that in my case, I was going to Hell. My name had already been sent down there and there was **nothing** I could do about it. Although I truly believed that our Creator no longer loved me, I still loved my Beloved deeply, despite my devastating plight.

Dean and I decided to go ahead and get married in the Presbyterian Church where his family belonged. The day of my wedding, as I walked down the aisle holding my father's arm, I silently cried. This was supposed to be the happiest day in my life, but looking ahead at the altar and the cross, I felt ugly and despicable. I perceived through my own belief that my Beloved was turning the Holy One's back on me. My Beloved did not want

to bless my marriage. Oh sure, we went through the motions of
the ceremony, but I was certain that my Beloved had severed the
relationship that we had with each other for all eternity. Deep
sorrow replaced the joy I should have experienced that beautiful
day. From that day forward until January 29, 1979, I would live
my life a fragmented being of the whole person I used to be.
Because I was not able to love myself, I felt unworthy of anyone
else's love, and I could not extend that love toward others. I
became perfectionistic, critical, demanding, and retributive. I
found no real purpose or meaning to my life. Life was good, but
there was no connection to the Divine that I once loved.

Through the ensuing years, I continued to firmly believe that
my Beloved no longer loved me. There was a tremendous void
in my soul. Several times I prayed asking my Beloved to forgive
me and love me again, but I never felt the nearness of our Creator as I once had. Abruptly, I would stop praying and reminded
myself that my Beloved did not want to listen to anything I had
to say. I was rotten to the core. Why would God want to hear
the aching words of my heart? I deserved the punishment I was
receiving I thought. My Beloved had cast me aside from His
heart because I failed to fulfill my responsibility as a good Christian by marrying a non-Catholic. This belief was firmly rooted
in my consciousness, and no one could convince me otherwise.
Years later and still missing the spiritual relationship I once had
with my Beloved, I decided that I would attempt to go to church
where I believed our Creator's presence to reside. I would beg
my Beloved to forgive me. In my mind however, I never felt that
God would listen to such a wretched person as I was.

One Sunday morning my courage surfaced, and I went to a
local Catholic church with just a shred of hope that my Beloved
would take me back to the Holy One's heart and love me again.
Walking down the aisle, my eyes began to scan the Holy arti-
facts, reminding me of the many years I had not been to church.
Taking my seat in a pew, I suddenly began to feel sick to my

altar. A red chair cushion was placed on the floor in front of the altar to use as a kneeling cushion when I was praying.

The idea of the May Altar was to bring my Beloved the gift of a fresh flower every day and place it upon the altar as a tangible expression of a little girl's love for her Heavenly Creator. It was something I wanted to do from the bottom of my heart. I would spend an hour on my knees on that red cushion, lost in time communing with my Beloved. Since we did not have our own flower garden, I would roam the neighborhood and ask our neighbors if I could pick just one flower for my May Altar. It must have been delightful for them to honor my request for I was never refused. Mother had always taught me to be kind to everyone I met, so it was very important that I respect their flower gardens once I received permission to pick my flower. After all, my neighbor was about to give me her most beautiful flower growing in her garden, so I always made sure I told the woman that God will be so pleased with her glorious flower placed on my May Altar.

Sometimes toward the end of May when the spring flowers were spent, I could not find a suitable flower to pick. My little heart was so heavy as if I were carrying the weight of the world on my small shoulders as I pondered what I should do. One day while I was walking with my head hanging so low it almost touched the ground, the answer came! There it was, stretching its golden flower head up between the blades of green grass and looking straight into my eyes as if to shout, "Pick me!" I caressed that tiny golden flower all the way home, and when I brought it to my May Altar, it seemed as if it were a perfect choice to give to my Heavenly Creator.

Mother laughed when she saw how I viewed the dandelion as a Divine Creation. It was perfect in my eyes, yet mother's perception was something different. A weed was something you weren't supposed to like. I didn't know what a weed was, I only knew that the golden flower matched the golden smile on my stomach. The words of the priest so many years earlier flooded my mind, reminding me that I was disobeying his orders. "Do not go to church anymore because you are not worthy to be in the presence of God's clean sanctuary. You are filth in his eyes. If you go to church, you will feel the wrath of God come upon you," I recalled him saying to me. The haunting memory of those words intensified my conviction that I was trespassing upon sacred territory. Those words began to churn over and over in my mind until my body could not take it any longer. I felt nauseated. I began to shake. The contempt I felt for myself was so strong that I convinced myself the priest had told me the truth. The physical symptoms I was experiencing while sitting in the pew were indicative that I was actually feeling the "wrath of God," or so I believed.

I could no longer remain in our Creator's house of worship. I was the worst human being on the face of the earth, and our Creator wanted no part of me. I absolutely and emphatically believed this! Hurriedly, I rose from the pew and bolted for the rear door. I would remove my despicable presence from our Creator's clean white sanctuary. Once outdoors, I vomited. That experience convinced me there was not a molecule of hope that my Beloved would love me. Hopelessness is a devastating feeling! From that moment on, I vowed I would never attempt under any circumstance to rebuild my relationship with my Beloved. However, **I never stopped loving our Creator deeply.** Looking back, I can't even remember harboring any negative feelings toward the priest or even toward our Creator. The only true anger, resentment, and blame I felt lay squarely upon my own self.

In retrospect, the priest was a good person, only looking out for my greatest good, the salvation of my soul. As a priest, that was his responsibility, and he did the best he knew at the time. Unfortunately, he chose fear to motivate me, as many at that time did, preaching hellfire and damnation. That caused a fear reaction in me, which is the opposite of love and which I would later learn, fear is not of our Creator.

Seventeen years would pass from the time the priest put the fear of God in me before my Beloved removed that fear and replaced it with the Light's life-transforming unconditional love!

CHAPTER 4

A NEW LIFE BEGINS

*Everything that is born of our Creator is Sacred and Holy.
Everything that happens is life's ever unfolding journey to
bring us home to our Beloved.*

During the birth of our first child in the 1960's, I had a near-death experience which I believe, served as a means of further preparing me for my actual union with our Creator during my mystical near-death-like experience in 1979. During my pregnancy, I was being monitored for eclampsia, a serious medical condition that was complicated by extreme high blood pressure, edema, and convulsions, with ensuing death. My physician was going to admit me to the hospital during my last month of pregnancy, but at the last moment, he decided against it telling me I would be okay.

Labor lasted thirty-nine grueling hours. I can remember the following events as if they happened yesterday. While I was on the delivery table, my spirit-body suddenly lifted out of my physical body and gently floated above my physical body to ceiling level where I became observant of the resusitation taking place below on Nancy's body. I saw "Nancy" below, but I had no feelings for that physical body lying on the table. It was as if I were looking at a coat that I no longer needed or wanted.

I felt complete and total detachment from the physical reality from which I had just transcended. My spirit-self entered a very dark void where I experienced tremendous bliss and peace that cannot be described using human language. Nothing was more important to me than experiencing the bliss and the reality that I had just entered. I wish I could use words to do justice to the bliss I was experiencing, but I cannot.

I was being drawn toward a very bright Light that was present in the dark void, and tremendous love was being beamed toward me like a lightening bolt of energy that lit up my spirit-self so that all I wanted was to go deeper into the Light. Nothing mattered but the Light and the love that I was experiencing during my blissful state. I was so enthralled to be in the Light's presence and so ecstatically happy to be moving toward the Light. I was being drawn like a magnet toward the Light as if the power of that attraction left me with no other choice than to go toward the Light of pure and perfect love. My whole spirit-being was lit with Light-awareness that this is where I was meant to go. Yes, the Light, the Light, only the Light, ONLY THE LIGHT!

My journey toward the Light, however, was suddenly interrupted when I heard the commotion of a nurse pounding on Nancy's physical body below screaming, "Come back, Nancy." She was pounding on Nancy's chest with her fist repeating, "Come back, Nancy, come back! You have a son!" she cried out in desperation.

A son? So what, I thought. This total emotional detachment for the physical realm, and everything in it was so extreme. Whatever was happening in the physical world had no interest for me, not even what was happening to my own physical body. Nothing mattered except going toward the Light. Nothing mattered but the love I was experiencing. Nothing mattered but this new reality I found myself in. At some level of awareness, I knew this is where I was meant to be, and any intrusion upon that journey to the Light was repulsive to me. I began to hate that nurse because her frantic voice was a major distraction to me. She was becoming an irritating **pest!** I recall thinking why didn't she shut up already? **I don't want to come back!** My thoughts and words were not being heard, and my frustration with that nurse who kept trying to call me back to my physical body was becoming more than I could bear. Finally, I was aggravated to the point where I finally gave in to the nurse's incessant, irritating voice and very reluctantly, I made the decision to stop her incessant nagging in the only way I could. Sadly, I made the decision to return to my physical body below, knowing that I was leaving the Light, leaving the love, leaving the bliss and peace that no words can adequately describe.

It still makes me sad to this day to remember that decision I made. But if I had made the decision not to return to physical life, I would not have been prepared by all the life experiences that I subsequently had which would then open my heart wider to be able to receive the Light's Grace year's later. I must thank that unknown nurse for being such a pest that I did make the decision to "come back" just as she wanted me to. Bless her wherever she is. Besides that, I have a son who was brought into the world on a Light-beam of Divine Love. How blessed I am!

After I made my decision to return to my physical body, the next thing I recall was waking up feeling very groggy. My tactile sensations began to inform my consciousness that I was lying on a cold metal surface and something was covering me from my toes to my head. Slowly regaining a little more conscious awareness, I recognized the covering as a sheet. With both my hands, I began very gently to uncover the sheet from my face. As I was doing that, I heard some noises in the room, but because I was laying flat and my eyes were looking upward toward the ceiling, the only thing I saw were bright white lights overhead.

I remember slowly turning my head to my right side, and I saw another figure lying motionless on a metal gurney the same way I was. A sheet was covering the entire body of that person

adjacent to where I was lying. I turned my head back to its original position once again looking at the ceiling when I suddenly
lost consciousness. It's funny how very specific memories can
linger in one's mind for over fifty years and still be so fresh that
those memories can bring one right back to that point in time as
they have for me.

What happened following the recall of the time I spent lying
on a cold metal gurney with a sheet covering me from head to toe
is something I immediately remembered as I once again regained
consciousness in my hospital room. My immediate thought was,
what happened to me? The thoughts and images of the delivery
room from the vantage point of ceiling level, the thoughts and
images of being in the presence of a Light who exuded such
tremendous unconditional love for me, the bliss and ineffable
peace, seeing and hearing the nurse pounding on my physical
body with her fist, shouting, "Come back Nancy, come back!"
was so vivid in my mind. I thought of the tactile sensations and
images of being covered with a sheet from head to toe lying on
a cold metal gurney, and the sight of seeing another body lying
on a gurney covered with a sheet from head to toe and lying
motionless next to me exactly as I had been lying. All these dis-
turbing memories came back to me in a flash the moment my
consciousness was fully restored after I had regained consciousness in my hospital room.

"Was that the morgue I woke up in?" I wondered. I knew
without second-guessing that what I experienced was very
REAL, not a figment of my imagination. There were so many
questions I wanted to ask my physician when he came to see me.
I realized very quickly however, that I would not tell him about
being out of my body for fear he would transfer me from the
maternity floor to the psychiatric ward. In the 1960's, the term
near-death experience had not yet been coined. I never heard of
anyone experiencing what I did, so I was very confused. I wanted
answers.

When my physician arrived, he was smiling warmly at me, and he asked how I felt. Not wasting a moment, I immediately interrogated him for some answers to my question, "What happened, what went wrong?" I asked. With a startled look in his eyes, he replied, "Nothing went wrong, nothing." I looked deeply into his eyes and said, "Yes, something did go wrong, and I want to know." He kept trying to dodge the questions, but I persisted in asking them. Finally, he put his arm around my shoulder and said, "Look, I am an excellent physician. Trust me. You want to have children again, don't you? he asked. Hmm, after thirty-nine grueling hours of labor I had to think about it for a moment, but I finally said "Yes." "Okay," he said. "I'm an excellent physician, and I'm afraid if I told you what happened it will do a lot of psychological damage, and you will never, ever want to have children again. So from this day forward, put this out of your mind. Don't look back. Forget what happened and move ahead with your life." I persisted in asking him what went wrong, but he would not discuss it any further with me. He left the room as abruptly as he arrived.

I knew no one would believe what I had experienced, so I decided to commit to secrecy concerning these events and move on with my life precisely what my physician told me to do. I didn't tell one person about my near-death experience or the circumstances regarding my recovery.

It wasn't until many years later when I had another Light encounter or near-death-like experience that resulted in ultimate union with our Creator that I began learning more about the reality of these experiences. I decided to have my medical records inspected to see what happened the day I had my near-death experience. My medical records indicate that I had a "normal" delivery and recovery and the records offer no "proof" that I was in any physical danger. However, my account as stated is the truth as I experienced it.

Why do you think my physician told me, *"I'm afraid if I*

told you what went wrong, it would cause such severe psychological damage that you would never, ever want to have children again?" That doesn't sound like a comment a physician would tell a patient who had a perfectly normal delivery does it?

I have my own opinion as to the reason my physician evaded my question of what went wrong that day. I am about to disclose something that readers may find hard to believe but I speak the truth.

During my prenatal visits, the nurse prepped me for the physician's exam and left to tell the physician that I was ready for him to attend to me. When my physician came into the exam room, I noticed that this time the nurse held a stop watch in her hand. When the door closed behind her, she started the clock. My doctor performed the exam, and when finished, he shouted to the nurse, "Stop!" She would then stop the stop watch. "What is the time?" he asked his nurse. "Twenty seven seconds," she replied. At that point, he would shout to his nurse, "How many times did I tell you to start the clock **as soon as the door closes.** You are wasting time! The poor nurse would almost cry because of his scornful attack upon her.

This happened every single time I went for my pre-natal visits. One day, I asked what he was doing and because of the short time he was examining me, I told him I didn't feel I was getting very good medical care. He put his arm around my shoulder (sound familiar?) and he told me that he was an excellent physician (sound familiar again?). He told me that he holds the record at the local hospital for doing C-Sections in under thirty seconds. He was now trying to do pre-natal exams in under twenty seconds!

I can only guess that while I was experiencing childbirth, something went wrong. It could have been the eclampsia and the poor pre-natal visits I had, or something went wrong due to physician negligence during the delivery. I will never know for sure, but I am certain that what happened that day happened exactly as I have written it. My proof is my own subjective experience. For others who need proof, I am sorry I am unable to provide you with it. For the skeptics, even proving one was dead doesn't erase the doubt of the actual experience itself, which can never be proven because it is a subjective experience. But we can learn to listen carefully to all these experiences because millions of people are telling us about them. In listening, we can learn to trust by faith that something is indeed happening to ordinary individuals worldwide. The focus of inquiry should not be centered upon the drama of the experiences themselves, but rather, we should wonder why are these experiences occurring at an accelerated rate during our present time, and **is there a message or meaning within these experiences surfacing that we humans need to pay attention to?** Is our Creator's voice discernable through near-death and similar mystical experiences? Yes, I believe so.

CHAPTER 5

FIRST WONDER, THEN DISCOVER

The voice of our soul is the intuitive faculty that our Beloved gave us to comprehend the mysterious ways in which Spirit moves.

When Dean and I moved to Columbus, Ohio, I worked as a cancer researcher and taught Cytology (study of cells) at Ohio State University for many years and later, I went into clinical work diagnosing in patients the early signs of tumor development and disease processes, remaining in this scientific field for thirty years. I was rigorously trained by the scientific method to define "reality" by what is observed through our physical senses; yet, my own near-death and near-death-like experiences transcend the boundaries of science. I am therefore, in an excellent position to be able to analyze my own subjective experiences from both a professional and experiential perspective. Having done this, there is one thing I know for certain, *there is an alternate transcendent reality which co-exists alongside our known physical reality, which is not governed by our physical laws.*

As I take you on this journey into the transcendent realities I have encountered, I hope that you will remember my scientific background and how convinced I am that alternate transcendent realities **do exist** even though science cannot *prove* they exist. It wasn't until my near-death-like or mystical experience in 1979 that I fully comprehended the role that the natural sciences play in teaching us about our own path in this exquisite realm of Creation. Nature reveals to us again and again that everything in Creation has a purpose and is based upon co-operation - completing and furthering one another. Every cell that is produced in any living entity adapts itself in shape and in every other way to fulfill the role assigned to it. Every cell has the built-in intelligence to reproduce and compels all its descendants to perform the identical function of the original cell. With exact precision the cells are in the right place where they belong forming your toes, nose, eyes and everything you need to function properly.

Imagine if our cells were not endowed with the instinct to be obedient to the great intent and design of our Creator. Trillions of cells without a master plan to adhere to could result in a human body where toenails are attached to eyebrows and eyes perched on the ends of big toes. Others might have their eyes located on their hips and others might not have eyes at all. But thank goodness there is order. Life pushes on building, repairing, and creating new life as an expression of Supreme Intelligence.

The tiny organelles in every cell act independently but are also part of the wholeness of the cell, which in turn, becomes part of the tissues. The tissues then form our organs, and we are finally made into a body. Every independent cell is like a sculptor who shapes all living things - the billowy weeping willow, the prickly cactus, and a child's beating heart. The inconceivable combination of all the elements necessary for the origin and maintenance of life is so marvelous that it takes my breath away, and I stand in awe before its Divine majesty.

Cells, so densely packed with assembly information, so elaborately detailed, are finely tuned machines that could not have originated by chance alone. At this level of science, there is the most astounding evidence on earth that there is a plan or purpose to life. Think about this.

Within our human bodies there are over one hundred trillion different cells. In each cell there is a nucleus that contains tightly wound strands of DNA, the genetic instructions necessary for sequencing amino acids in proteins in the organism. DNA has about three billion different pieces of information. Each piece can have four combinations. When you multiply those four combinations by the three billion pieces of information, it's absolutely mind-boggling! Let's take this a step further. There are few combinations of that DNA that allows a human to perform its function relative to the immense probabilities and different combinations of DNA within the cell; so if you take the number of ways you could arrange the DNA to produce a human and the number of possible ways, the odds are staggering that it would happen by chance.

At the cellular level, nature teaches us that every organic form of life has individuality, yet is part of a greater order. If we think of man as an independent entity just as the independent cell, we can begin to see that man is also part of a greater order just as everything that exists from elementary particles to atoms and molecules, to the primordial mix of stars, solar systems, and galaxies. Each part contributes its individuality because without it the whole organism would lose its configuration and collapse. At the same time, each part must co-operate with the demands of the whole in order to maintain the balance of the hierarchy. In 1994, the Nobel Prize in Medicine was awarded to Alfred G. Gilman and Martin Rodbell for their discovery of "G-Proteins" and the role of these proteins in signal transduction in cells. In simple words, cells communicate with each other through their cell walls.

If we can fully grasp this cellular communication inwardly, the easier it will be for us to recognize that there is a higher purpose to our existence which is indestructibly imprinted on the human spirit and which will ultimately lead us to the knowledge that man is a vehicle for Divine Expression. We can realize and utilize the Infinite Wisdom, which our Creator has created for our use so that we can try to bring to the world some part of the Divine Light and manifest the spiritual realm that corresponds to our species. Each of us, contributing our bits and pieces to enable the whole of mankind to come into our Divine Inheritance, will help widen our understanding and help us reach the heights of enlightenment, which our Beloved has conceived as a means of human destiny.

CHAPTER 6

A RARE GIFT

Embrace and cherish the beauty and importance of friendships. Each has its connection to the Divine. Each one opens us up like the golden sunlight that unfolds the delicate petals of a fragrant rose.

Fate has a way of bringing together those individuals destined to impact our lives. During the time Dean was attending OSU in the early sixties, he met a classmate, John, who quickly became our best friend. In fact, our relationship with John and his wife Jean developed into such a close loving bond that we thought of ourselves as family instead of best friends. We felt like brothers and sisters, and we loved their children as our own. Everyone should have sometime in their lives, the kind of loving tie to someone like we had with John and Jean. It is a precious gift that best friends give to one another, and a gift that remains forever in one's memory, never to be forgotten. John's impact would be the spiritual catalyst for my mystical encounter with our Creator just a few days after his death in 1979.

John and his family decided to move to Alaska for several years. John, an avid outdoors man, longed for a sense of adventure and closeness to nature that wasn't comparable to anything else in the lower states. The letters and taped recordings they sent us of the life they were living in Anchorage sounded thrilling to us. When they asked us to visit them for several weeks, we decided to go. John had planned something we would never forget. Our sons were excited beyond words. Dean, also a nature enthusiast, couldn't wait for the trip to begin. So off to Alaska we all went in the summer of 1976.

The plan was to fly from Copper Center with an Alaskan guide in his small twin-engine plane deep into the untamed wilderness to spend a week living with nature, two hundred miles from the nearest road. We would leave civilization and all its comforts behind to experience a once-in-a-lifetime opportunity.

To say I was reluctant to go would be an understatement. I was *terrified!* Thoughts of bears, moose, and other wild creatures roaming the forests that we would inhabit frightened me intensely. John and Dean were always reassuring me that everything would be all right, but it didn't help much. Fearful thoughts held me captive. I could not think of anything else. What would I do if I saw a bear approaching me? I imagined being pounced upon by thick razor-like claws ripping at my flesh, my body slowly being devoured by this hideous beast. Worse still, what would I do if I witnessed this ghastly scene of carnage happening to my husband, my sons, or John and his family? Deep in the wilderness, two hundred miles from the nearest road was not something I could be relaxed about.

Once we got there, however, my fears subsided. Instead, John's sense of the beauty and wonder of our Beloved's creation began to take hold of my own thoughts. Never before in my life did I see such beauty. John taught my own eyes to see what John loved so much. A deep, abiding sense of union, a connection between earth and man seemed to capture my inner being, and I was captivated by the essence of life surrounding all of us. The cold, crystal clear glacier stream became our source of drinking water. I have never tasted water so cold, pure, and delicious in all my life even though I was sharing its refreshment with a nearby squirrel. For a moment, as my eyes made contact with the squirrel's eyes, I wondered if I was the first human being, the squirrel had ever seen. I was after all, occupying a place in his world where humans don't reside. I felt deeply honored to share his world with him for that captivating moment.

The duration of that trip was spent living closer to nature than I had ever experienced in my entire life. Prior to that trip, I rarely contemplated the natural world in any meaningful way. Trees, birds, mountains, flowers, and streams were simply background objects that, of course I noticed, but I was emotionally detached from them. I had been a city girl for the first thirty years of my life and had no real desire to discover what I would now say is the awesome masterpiece that continually springs forth from the Creator's artistic palette. There is a great lesson we can learn from nature if we open our eyes and our hearts to see and hear its message. Nature lives in harmony with itself, always renewing itself so it gives back to itself what is needed for its continued survival. Nature respects us by providing for our needs as well, but we must also return that respect to nature and tend to her needs.

I believe the majestic beauty that I was beginning to absorb deep within the very essence of my being awakened a part of my spiritual consciousness. This awakening helped contribute to the unfolding of my higher self that ultimately came to fruition during my near-death-like, mystical encounter two years later. I learned the importance of respecting the environment that we share with all life from John during that wilderness trip. John and Jean left Alaska to move back to their home in Ohio about a year later. He left his Cessna airplane behind and planned one day to return to Anchorage and fly it back to Ohio. That decision was made in January 1979, the month and year my entire life would change and never be the same again.

One evening, I had a dream about John piloting his aircraft over the Alaskan glaciers. I was an observer in the dream looking at John from the outside of his left side window. He was elated flying his plane over the rugged mountains he loved so dearly; the expression on his face revealed his joy. Suddenly, his facial features took on a tortured, panicked expression as he began to touch and adjust the controls on the plane. Something was wrong, very wrong. Visibility ahead was no longer possible. All he could see was vast, bright whiteness above and below him.

He was frantically trying to regain control over his plane, but it was not responding to his efforts. In the final moments, realizing the futility of his efforts, he turned his head to the left side window and looked at me with such a loving expression in his teary eyes and cried out, "Nancy," just before the plane crashed into the thick, white snow below. In my dream, I did not observe if he survived the crash. At that point, I awoke. It was 6:00 a.m. Immediately, I sensed from deep within my gut that the dream was prophetic, and my friend had died. An hour later Jean telephoned me to tell me his plane crashed just thirty minutes out of Anchorage. He had been killed. Over the next several days, my family and I were grief-stricken. We just lost a member of our extended family.

CHAPTER 7

MYSTERIOUS WRITING

Our Beloved does not hide anything from us that can be used for our ultimate good for all. We understand the unknowable by Divine Illumination revealed by Divine Loving Grace.

The process of opening up to something greater than one's self began when Jean asked me to deliver a eulogy for John's funeral service. I insisted that I could not do such a thing. After all, I was emotionally upset. I couldn't stand up in front of all those people and speak in a well-composed manner. I certainly didn't want to make anyone uncomfortable with my own grief.

Jean was very insistent about me delivering his eulogy since we were like brothers and sisters. "Please," she said, "You write so beautifully, you are the perfect one to deliver it." We argued back and forth with one another, Jean pleading and me refusing. "I have an idea," she said. "Couldn't you at least write the eulogy, and then I'll give the eulogy to the minister for him to deliver? she asked. "Well, that sounded non-threatening to me. Yes, I could do that. I accepted the offer.

I still had a few days before the funeral service, so I put the writing of the eulogy out of my mind. My immediate focus was on comforting Jean and her sons and spending as much time with them as I could. Finally, I could no longer procrastinate over the eulogy. The funeral was the next day. I had to write the eulogy. In my bedroom with notepad and pen in hand, I tried to write something, but nothing happened. I had writer's block. How do I write a eulogy? I never wrote one before. How would I put his life into some written form that would be meaningful to his family and friends? I sat, waiting for inspiration to come, but nothing happened. Intuitively, I felt that I was in the wrong setting to write the eulogy. Perhaps if I went somewhere else, I could write it. Where? I thought. That still small voice within told me to pick up my notepad and pen and tell my family I had no idea where I was going, but I had to go somewhere else to write. I told them not to worry, I would be okay, and I would return after I wrote the eulogy.

I didn't have the foggiest idea where I was intending to go as I was driving my car. Grief-filled thoughts of John flooded my mind; tears poured from my eyes. *How could this be happening?* I wondered. John is only 39 years old. There were so many plans both our families had to share together. We were supposed to grow old together, and when our memories started to fail, our sons would tell us the stories of the "good old days" when we all went to Alaska together as a family. Or, on future camping excursions we had planned, we would sit around the campfire while the fireflies danced toward the light of the fire and cautiously flirt with us; laughter and joy would fill the night air as we shared our loving friendship with one another. "It isn't fair!" I shouted.

Aimlessly wandering throughout the country roads turning one way then another, I drove my car toward a densely wooded area. I stopped and got out. With pen and notepad in hand, I walked toward the woods still numb from the reality of John's sudden death. There, by a small babbling stream was a large limestone boulder on which I gingerly perched. Immediately, I felt a peaceful, serene feeling fall upon me. The cold January air seemed to disappear as if I were no longer conscious of the chill that only moments ago pierced the thin raincoat I wore.

A feeling of John's spiritual presence beside me startled me. My visual perception did not observe any shape or form of John. Yet, **I knew** beyond my discerning intellect that what I was sensing deep within my inner self was true. My analytical brain was always trying to steer me away from my true feelings within with scolding words like, "This can't be. John is dead. There has to be an explanation for this." I reasoned that my mind was playing tricks on me; yet at the same time, I knew that I was experiencing something very **REAL!** When I acknowledged my friend's presence, I felt totally relaxed and at peace. Only when my intellect and analytical side dominated by attempting to judge that moment, did I feel confused and startled.

This would be the spot where I would write the eulogy. It felt right. I let my thoughts flow with the inner awareness of John's spirit beside me. Warmth and peace permeated my inner being as I opened my notebook to begin writing the eulogy. What happened next was something for which I was not prepared; something that would forever remind me that there is a very thin veil separating this world from the otherworldly dimension. The moment my pen touched the notepaper, my hand began to move very rapidly across the lines of the paper. Words were forming on the paper, but the words were all connected to one another. There were no pauses for beginning of new sentences, capital letters or punctuation marks.

Astonished at the way my hand was moving so rapidly, I did not realize the content of what I was writing until after the text had been completed. Mentally, I did not associate any thinking process with writing the text. The words were forming faster than I could think of them in my head. Normally, I write a letter for instance, by first thinking of the words in my mind, and then I write the words. In this instance however, the words on the paper were being written faster than my mind was discerning them. In fact, my mind was actually preoccupied with thoughts of awe and bewilderment of the writing process unfolding at that time. At last, when the pen in my hand suddenly stopped, I looked down upon the pages of text before me, words all connected to one another, and I began to decipher the meaning by placing periods at the end of sentences, and correcting beginning of sentences with capital letters.

"Oh my goodness! This was the eulogy," I realized. How could this be possible? It began with words and a writing style totally unfamiliar to me. The remaining text captured John's essence and spoke of the values he was leaving behind for his sons. After the funeral service Jean informed me that the beginning of the eulogy was John's favorite passage from Kahill Gibran's book, *The Prophet*. At that time in my life, I had never heard of Kahill Gibran or his book, The Prophet, much less be able to recite verbatim, a passage from it. The passage that appeared on the eulogy read as follows:

"Much have we loved you. But speechless was our love, and with veils has it been veiled. Yet now it cries aloud unto you, and would stand revealed before you. And ever has it been that love knows not its own depth until the hour of separation."

Realizing that something of tremendous significance occurred during those moments that I spent sitting on that rock beside the stream, I could no longer deny that my mind was playing tricks on me. Something very **REAL** happened that I didn't fully understand, but I knew I didn't have to understand it in order to accept its reality.

I decided I would not tell my family about the way the eulogy was written for fear of being labeled crazy. When I arrived home, I read the eulogy to them, and they were deeply touched by it. I wanted to acknowledge that I didn't write it but then decided it was better left unsaid. In my heart, I knew that I did not consciously write it, and to this day I will still insist it was not I. Who? I cannot answer that question. Perhaps the answer can be found in the meeting I had with John's minister the night before I wrote the eulogy.

During the last viewing at the funeral home, the minister approached me and said, "I understand you will be writing the eulogy, and I will be reading it for you tomorrow during the funeral service." "Yes," I replied. "Would you do a favor for me?" I asked the minister. "Would you please say a prayer for me so I can write the eulogy because God won't listen to me if I prayed, but I know God will listen to you because you are a minister in good favor with God." With a somewhat puzzled look upon his face, he replied, "Of course I will pray for you."

Void of any spiritual life at that time, I believed that I was the last person whose prayers God wanted to listen to, let alone, answer. Do you see a possible connection to my prayer request and the manner in which the eulogy evolved? Was there a possible spiritual process unfolding that allowed me to become receptive to the outpouring of text that comprised John's eulogy? Was it the result of a minister's petition on my behalf to our Creator that helped open a channel or means of communication to me from the spiritual realm? I believe so. The Creator works in mysterious ways, and Spirit's voice can be heard in the silent written words as well as responding to someone's sincere prayers. There is indeed, power in prayer. Since I was not intending to deliver the eulogy at John's funeral service the next day, there was no need for me to become familiar with its contents by rehearsing the text. The minister was going to read it, so I simply typed the eulogy and set it aside for the next day.

CHAPTER 8

THE AWAKENING

To know our Beloved is to awaken to know the full ecstatic essence of one's being.

The next morning was January 29, 1979, the day my entire life changed instantaneously. Relieved that I didn't have to deliver the eulogy, my family and I went to the funeral service held in the chapel of the funeral parlor. The organ music played softly in the background as everyone gathered to greet John's family and friends. The chapel was filled to capacity, and inwardly, I smiled as I thought of the heartfelt imprint his life made upon so many people.

Roses, carnations, and gladiolas perfumed the air with an intoxicating aroma that swept through the entire funeral chapel. Jean, her eyes red and swollen from long agonizing days of crying, approached me and asked, "Do you have the eulogy? The minister isn't here yet so keep it until he arrives; then I'll come and get it from you." I nodded my head and said, "Okay."

Mingling and talking with others about fifteen minutes before the beginning of the funeral service, I suddenly began to experience a very powerful burst of energy beginning from my toes and moving rhythmically up my calves, knees, abdomen, spine, neck and exiting the top of my head. Years later, I would learn this was a kundalini awakening. When this tremendous feeling of energy exited, instantaneously, I felt light and was buoyant as if helium balloons were attached to my shoulders. My grief was suddenly replaced with an unearthly peace and an acceptance of John's death. The peace I felt cannot be described in words. Perhaps the best words ever written to describe this tremendous peace are, *"I am leaving you with a gift -peace of mind and heart! And the peace I give isn't fragile like the peace the world gives."* (John 14:27)

Once again Jean approached me and told me that the minister had arrived. "Where's the eulogy?" she asked. I said, "Oh no, I have to be the one to deliver the eulogy." Confused, she said, "What do you mean? We went through all of this before. You said you couldn't handle it." I replied, "Yes I can. In fact, **I have to be the one to deliver it.**"

The words were coming from my mouth as if a wiser part of me were speaking. I had no conscious idea why I said it had to be me. The words simply spilled out that way because a deep all-knowing feeling from within urged me to say those words. Up until that very moment, I was intent upon giving the minister the eulogy to read. In retrospect, I believe I acted entirely on the prompting of Spirit's voice within.

Moments later, I heard the minister call my name to deliver the eulogy. Responding to his call, I started to walk toward the lectern, and just before approaching it, once again, I sensed John's spirit beside me. I felt my right hand being placed in his. Reacting to his "presence," I turned my head to my right side as if to acknowledge his presence with me. The vision of his presence with me was not coming from my physical eyes, but rather from another source that was somehow connected to my own supernatural or spiritual consciousness. I was absolutely convinced that he was standing right beside me holding my hand and giving me the assurance that he was very much alive, albeight in a different form. However at this point, the logical, analytical side of me started to capture my attention with doubting thoughts. *Nancy, wait a minute. You know where you are. You know John is lying in the coffin beside you. You know he is dead, so why are you "seeing and feeling" his presence with you?*

Puzzled by this heightened awareness, I told myself there was no time to think about what was happening. I had to deliver the eulogy, and I decided that when everything was over, I would have plenty of time to convince myself there was a logical explanation for what I was experiencing. Perhaps it's wish fulfillment, not wanting John to be dead, so my mind was playing tricks on me. Reassuring myself that I would deal with the matter later, I continued walking toward the lectern.

Since I wasn't very familiar with the contents of the eulogy, I decided that I was simply going to read the text as written. Carefully placing the paper on the lectern, my eyes touched the eyes of the large number of people gathered together to honor John's memory. Sadness gripped the room full of family and friends gathered together to bid farewell to a wonderful human being. My eyes connected with Jean's tearing eyes as I imagined the immense stamina that she had to endure in order to get to this intolerable day when she would bury her beloved husband.

My own body continued to remain unremittingly calm ever since that moment I experienced that mysterious unearthly peace fifteen minutes earlier. Fear and anxiety were nonexistent. I proceeded to read the first three sentences of the eulogy when suddenly my eyes lifted from the paper and were drawn toward the back left side of the room at ceiling level. Immediately, I saw a brilliant, pure radiating white Light unlike anything I have ever seen upon the earth. It was not sunshine or light coming from lighting fixtures. For one thing, the room we were in had no windows. Second, I recognize all sorts of lighting fixtures and the light they produce, and believe me, it was not light that any of us have ever seen on this planet!

Looking at the Light, it became brighter and brighter, glistening like crystal reflecting the sun's rays. The brilliance illuminated my eyes to unparalleled luminosity, yet it didn't hurt my eyes one bit. Imagine for a moment, looking directly at a trillion suns that have merged into one, and that you are able to look at it without squinting your eyes and being absolutely comfortable with its radiance. In our limited awareness, we have difficulty even imagining what that might be like. The illumination of the Light that I was seeing was infinite and without end.

Immediately, when I looked at the Light within my consciousness, there was an instantaneous recognition of **who** the Light was. **This was the same Light that I experienced during my near-death experience during childbirth. I was in the presence of the Holy Light again!** Deep within the total existence of my being, every cell in my body *awakened* with the recognition of the Light's glorious presence. When I cast my eyes upon the Divine Presence before me, ecstasy and bliss permeated my entire being with the explosive energy of love, gratitude, awe, reverence, and humility.

Let me interrupt the story for a moment and explain that during the entire duration of the eulogy, the physical body and brain of "Nancy" was engaged in the physical act of delivering the eulogy in front of the people gathered to hear it. Another part of my consciousness which I recognized as the **real true essence of me** (my spirit or soul), had somehow transcended the constraints of my physical body and had lifted it out. I was experiencing a more **REAL** dimension than the physical reality my physical body was inhabiting at the time. As I continue with my story, be reminded that as time was taking place in the physical reality; time was totally absent in the Heavenly reality in which I had entered. In order for me to communicate my experience, I have to use linear time to convey its message. I have to structure words to form sentences, and it will take time for you to read them. However, time was absent during my experience. Every event, every thought, every word communicated - everything was happening at the same moment. A tremendous amount of information was being integrated into my consciousness without linear time getting in the way. Let me continue on with the story now.

There are no human words to describe what I experienced with the Light; still, I must try to communicate my rather feeble words so you can attempt to understand what I am trying to say. As my eyes were beholding the luminous energy of the Light and my entire being pulsated with ecstasy as I acknowledged the presence of the Holy One, the Light moved toward me and flooded me with an outpouring of pure, Divine, unconditional love beyond human comprehension. Infinite and perfect love was being infused into the very recesses of my being. Every nook and cranny of my being was bombarded with what seemed to be a nuclear explosion of unconditional love.

The boundless power of Divine Love continued to permeate my body, mind, and soul as the Light continued to move toward me. As the Light encircled me, I began to feel the motion of being caught up in a whirlpool, gently, yet powerfully, beginning to blend and merge into the whole in a spirally, upward path. All the while, I felt safe, loved, and cradled like a newborn in the arms of its mother. Fear was non-existent in the Light's presence.

The ego, "I," Nancy, was seemingly transforming from a separate identity into Divine Radiance. The Light and I became one. Truth was absolute for me. I understood that the Light and the unconditional love that originated from the Light was the essential nature of reality. Let me reiterate, that in the presence of the Light, pure truth exists. Deception and ambiguity are totally non-existent. All knowledge entering my consciousness was **truthful** to its core.

The moment I lifted out of my body, instantaneously, I realized that I had transcended from a physical world of **illusion** and had entered into the **REAL** reality. Flooded with joy, my soul knew that I was "home" again, the true place of my real existence with the Light. Then in a momentary pause of sadness, I thought of the non-believers, and the scientists who refused to accept the possibility that another dimension exists beyond the physical sense time reality because it couldn't be observed, measured, or reproduced in any way. I can't begin to describe my feelings of compassion and empathy that I felt for them. My whole being ached when I thought of the time when they themselves would enter this spiritual Heavenly dimension after death and discover that they had disbelieved in a Supreme Reality, and it was there **ALL THE TIME!** The beauty and simplicity of our true nature was overwhelming to me. I pondered the question, why do we always make everything so complicated? It was so **simple!**

Able to observe the surroundings below me, my spirit-self floated around the room like a gentle snowflake effortlessly traveling its intended path. The people I noticed were watching "Nancy" delivering the eulogy. No longer did I see people as strangers to me in the physical realm, I was now seeing them in their true form, as I was. They were all beings of spiritual **Light** at the core of their being. Their human body was simply a protective covering that is used to enable the soul to function well in the physical realm. But in the spiritual realm there is no need for covering of any kind, for the purity of our being is *Light*.

As I continued to observe the people in the room, my love for them poured from the heart of my soul for I realized that we are all one. All conscious thoughts and insights that manifested throughout my experience took place through a telepathic process. I was given the answers to my questions by placing them directly into my consciousness as soon as my thoughts surfaced. I never felt the need to question or doubt the knowledge I received because I knew that the Light was offering me the truth.

Moving upward with the Light through the chapel ceiling, above the building, the city streets, the state, the country, the planet, and moving at a tremendous rate of speed, we moved into the dark universe above. All the while I was merged into oneness with the Light, and everything that occurred felt comfortable, natural, and truthful. We stopped traveling after we reached what seemed to me to be the center of the universe. I looked around and was awestruck at the multidimensional cosmos before me. It was no longer a four-dimensional reality as I was accustomed to, but rather, many dimensions. I "saw" at least eleven, but the word "saw" can be misleading.

I do not have the words to convey what I observed because I don't believe our scientific terminology has been empowered with the vocabulary yet because to date, science has not yet discovered or proven what I saw. The closest I can come to describing it would be higher energy dimensions. Instead of "seeing" them as individualized places, it would be more correct to say that they were all intermingled with one another, yet distinct from one another. I know this doesn't make sense to you. But I cannot describe this aspect of my experience for it is like asking me to describe a color for you. I can't. For the time being, I will have to rest with the ineffability of that particular journey.

However, it is my understanding that the new quantum theoretical physicists state that all our knowledge about the absoluteness of our physical reality may be wrong. Quantum physicists in leading universities around the world are seriously investigating what mystics have long suggested that our world is an illusion. If you recall, the moment I lifted out of my physical body, I realized that I had just left an **illusionary reality** and had entered into the **REAL** reality. I had no previous knowledge about quantum physics at that time in my life nor did I ever entertain the idea that we live in an illusionary world. I would have laughed if someone told me this world is an illusion. But that is exactly what I experienced!

The implications that there is no one reality but many, and that the role of consciousness plays a part in creating multiple realities could radically change our understanding of our physical universe. For those interested in learning more about this rapidly changing perspective of our physical reality held by theoretical quantum physicists, I would highly recommend the book, *"The Elegant Universe,"* and *"The Fabric of the Cosmos,"* written by Brian Greene, Professor of physics and mathematics at Columbia University.

Now, let's return to my experience. Merged into oneness with the Light, we began to travel at a tremendous speed once again deeper and deeper into the dark universe until the Light and I reached the beginning of the creation of the universe. I was observing the Light of God as the Supreme and sole Creator of the universe, and I understood that the Light was the starting point of everything ever created. To my amazement, I learned that the Light was living energy- the sum total of and infinite energy of the created and uncreated cosmos. Until that very moment, that knowledge had not been part of my belief system. I had always envisioned our Creator to be a man with a long white robe and a white beard. The Creator that I encountered was an infinite loving Being of Light energy that cannot be conceptualized. It proved to me that humanity has an extremely limited view of who or what the Creator is. However, to help us imagine what the Creator might be, it is reasonable to think of the Creator in a way that makes the Creator's image perceptible and individually meaningful to us.

The Creator showed me that the very first created form emerged from Divine Light as a spark of that same Light, and that all of Creation - everything - from the atoms, molecules, quarks, has at its core the spark of Divine Light, which is a very pure and perfect form of *Divine energy, or Divine Love.* Its power is greater than our limited awareness can imagine or comprehend. I had a vision of seeing humankind in its current evolutionary state of being, symbolized spiritually as being in the caveman era. Just as the caveman discovered the energy and power of fire and ultimately evolved to a higher state of being, I saw that humankind today has the potential to discover lying within themselves, the ultimate energy and power of Divine Light and Love. Discovering and utilizing this knowledge would be the catalyst for a new evolutionary world where Heaven on earth will be realized. This knowledge was a profound insight with which the Light was blessing me. I thought all we have to do is to *awaken* to the realization of who we are at the core of our being which is Light and Love, and to express that outwardly, unconditionally into the world. That message resonated loud and clear. I understood that was the bottom line. That was humankind's destination.

Once again, I began to feel a sense of rapid movement as the Light and I began to travel back toward earth. All the while I felt one with the Light. Peace, love, truth, and knowledge followed me wherever we went. We stopped as the earth came into view. From a distance above, I marveled at the spectacular, exquisite sight before my eyes. Divine Love was flooding my consciousness as I recognized the gift of life below. With that, the Light gave me a most incredible gift. All during my experience, the Light and I were merged into oneness. The feelings I was experiencing were identical to the feelings of the Holy One. Feelings about conditional love and my ego need to judge, question, and doubt were gone.

Closer, we moved toward earth, and I was allowed to see all the social injustices, the wars, the murderers, the chaos and disorder. Although this will sound bizarre, I felt there was indeed order. Not mankind's order, but Divine order among the chaos. I was observing without condemnation, judgment, anger or hatred, the thieves, the drunkards, the diseased. The Light was exuding unconditional love for everyone, and everything below, and my own consciousness reflected the same.

I understood at my soul level that everything was working out the way it was supposed to. Yes, even the worst kind of tragedy. I cannot articulate this in any way to prevent anyone from regarding this as ludicrous and sheer nonsense. We live in a world that conditions us to respond to negative situations in a negative way. We have not yet learned to live lives of unconditional love, a love that says, "I will love you **no matter what!**" This does not mean that you love the *behavior* if it is bad. It does mean that you can still love the pure, innocent *core* of that person's being. The Light of God recognizes the Light of God in others through the rays of Divine-given lucidity that reaches deep within our souls. When our ego attachments have been transcended to the state where we recognize our true connection to our Beloved, then and only then, can we fully begin to understand this.

As we began traveling once again at a tremendous rate of speed, the Light and I passed by every person on the face of the earth. I was bursting with unconditional love for everyone, no strings attached, even though I was witnessing some horrific scenes of social injustices. As I said earlier, I understood that everything was working out the way it was supposed to, ultimately to fit into some larger plan. I had the impression that each person was playing his/her role, and that it affected the whole. Without that part, the whole would be incomplete. Like a picture puzzle, each part was uniquely an integral and important aspect. Missing, the entire picture would then be disrupted. There was underlying **spiritual good** to be found in **all** things.

During this portion of my encounter with the Holy Light, there was an intense revelation on which I focused. I began to understand the meaning of unconditional love. In spite of all the chaos on the earth, our Beloved loved everyone equally. I **absolutely understood that each person is intimately cherished beyond human comprehension.** My own consciousness was completely devoid of all ego boundaries. In that state of blissful unity with the Light, I felt ecstatic with the knowledge that I was viewing the earth and its inhabitants from my true being, my soul.

Words can never express the mystery of Divine unconditional love, and the soul's unitive consciousness with the Infinite Being. It can never be described; it can only be experienced. Think of a beautiful song being played by an orchestra. The thinking mind will use words to describe the music, but that is only an attempt to define it. When you listen to the orchestra playing, you are aware of what you are feeling or experiencing. The inner feeling may be delightful, or it may be unpleasant. In any case, you know what the inner experience of the music feels like. Think of our Beloved as the music itself minus the orchestra, and you will have a better understanding of something that is indefinable.

After experiencing the unconditional love for everyone on earth, the Light focused attention on me. In a sanctified embrace of total unconditional Holy Love, I was given a life review. As you recall in earlier chapters, I described having lived a life of highly successful accomplishments as a fashion model, winner of 30 beauty contests, dancer, and medical cytologist. My competitive nature allowed me to reap the reward of notoriety, respect, privilege, and monetary gain of which I was grateful. My ego had served me well and had motivated me to accomplish many extraordinary things with my life that brought me great pleasure.

Now, in the presence of the Light of God, I was having my life reviewed. Contrary to what my prior religious beliefs had been of God judging me, I was in charge of judging myself while the Light of God loved me unconditionally throughout this review. Loving Grace exceeded any desire for justice. Every ego-motivated experience in my life was reviewed with detachment and indifference as if those events were irrelevant in the scheme of things. To my shocking discovery, my life review primarily focused on the times when I did not love others as well as myself. My soul understood that only LOVE was the measuring stick of our lives, not the accomplishments, social status, monetary gain, etc.

I was shown a very thin, wispy veil, so thin a breath of air could have disintegrated it. I stood on one side of the veil and on the other side was the Light. The veil represented the barrier, which prevented me from realizing my true nature. I was shown that the purpose of our lives was simply to remove that veil by spiritually growing in unconditional love. Every life experience that I had in which I embraced guilt, fear, self-condemnation and unloving feelings toward myself or others, represented taking giant steps away from the veil I was supposed to remove. Every time I expressed love in any way, I took a giant step *toward* the veil.

Apparently my life, following my spiritual crisis, had been a succession of giant steps away from the veil. My low self-esteem forced me to become a perfectionist, and I saw that the reason I wanted to be the best wife, mother, career woman, and community volunteer was because I needed to love myself. The resentments that I felt for others who did not live up to my expectations were simply resentments that I had for myself. I realized that I had expected others to make me happy instead of discovering my own true happiness and the Divine Life that lies within.

The Light also made it crystal clear to me that all the while I had lived my life believing that my Beloved no longer loved me, it was **NOT TRUE!** In fact, throughout my entire life, from beginning to end, our Creator's love for me was *unchangeable.* It was the first time I truly understood what unconditional love meant. All the while, I held onto the false belief that I was a rotten human being incapable of being loved by our Creator, my Beloved was right there, loving me and cherishing me the way I was. I had a mistaken perception of myself.

It was at that moment that I felt **tremendous remorse** for the way I had determined to know the mind of our Creator and judged myself to be unworthy in our Creator's eyes for all those years. I felt so sorry and apologetic for my false beliefs and the self-separation it caused in the relationship between my Beloved and me. Through the intimate understanding of our Creator's unchanging love for me, I knew that our Creator's love was not human love, the kind that changes and is rewarded only when good acts are performed.

I was instructed to remove the veil and as I did, I saw that I was a reflection of the Light in the image of the Holy Light. At that instant, I felt exhilarated to realize that I finally had recognized my true self. Once I affirmed this truth about myself, I was shown a symbol which solidified my understanding of my Beloved's unconditional Love for me and **everyone else**. Symbolically, I was shown a big black chunk of coal which represented the dark, ugly, and worthless way I felt about myself during the period in my life when I was swallowed up in the illusion of my false self. The Light however, showed me the image the Light always had for me. That image symbolically appeared as a brilliant, perfect diamond!

Let me explain the analogy. Both coal and diamonds are made of the same material, carbon. Coal is subjected to intense pressures and heat within the earth until all the impurities have been driven out of it. Once that takes place, it becomes a precious gem, or diamond. It was as if our Creator had no other eyes to see through other than through the eyes of unconditional love. Through my Beloved's eyes, I was a precious gem, just the way I was! I felt like the Roto-Rooter man had just made a house call and had cleaned out my blocked-up pipes. All the worthless impurities that constituted the image of my false self were released, and now, the priceless gem of my *true loving self* could radiate its brilliance and flow uninhibited throughout the pipes in my *"new house."*

With the tenderness of a nurturing father's love, the Light allowed me to empty myself of all negative self-imagery, so I was restored to wholeness in the image of the Holy Light. I cherish that gift with all my heart and soul. I will never again choose to assume the illusion of my false self no matter what the circumstance. If I make bad mistakes or hurt someone, it is not intentional. I can now recognize the error of my judgment, make amends, learn from the mistake, pick myself up, and move on without punishing myself in the process.

Because our Creator loves us unconditionally, it does not mean for one moment that we are entitled to display behavior that is inconsistent with our true spiritual nature and that our Creator will approve of those actions. Our Creator understands the regrets we have when we make foolish mistakes. The Holy One understands the pain we feel when we hurt someone and feel twinges of guilt every time we stir up memories of the bad things we did or others did to us. Guilt hurts us deeply and causes us to live in the ego, which is an illusion. Only love is real. When we truly feel loved and cherished in spite of our mistakes, we long to act in **loving**, not unloving ways. It is our attempt to return our love to the One who loves us so much. It becomes natural for us to respond lovingly because we also cherish the kind of love that forgives our transgressions.

Think for a moment of a special pet you are blessed to have. In your pet's heart, you are cherished with the rare love that is unconditional. Your pet overlooks your faults; it doesn't care about your weight, your bald head, or the size of your bank account. It just wants to be near you, snuggle close beside you, sharing the warmth of your touch and gentle voice. Doesn't that kind of love cause a reaction deep within you to act outwardly toward your pet in loving ways? It would be unthinkable for you to abuse your beloved pet, wouldn't it? To many of us, we love them so much we consider them a member of our own family. Realizing this may be an overly simplistic example, but it is the only way I can compare the kind of response an individual has when shown the beautiful gift of unconditional love. I am convinced that our pets come straight from our Beloved's Light to teach us what unconditional love is and what our lives could be like when we become that love ourselves.

Remember, I said earlier that all communication was taking place telepathically and that time was absent. A tremendous amount of knowledge was being transferred from the Light directly into my consciousness. I was like a dry sponge soaking up every morsel of spiritual truth that my Great Teacher was revealing to me so that I would understand that truth and live it. The basis of this book is that knowledge that came from my Great Teacher as the Light's loving gift to you.

The fruit of love is forgiveness, and the root of forgiveness is love. Love is our birthright. It is the inner core of our being, the actual Light of our Beloved. When we are ready to forgive others and ourselves for past behaviors that bind us to the illusion of our false selves, we heal ourselves and free ourselves from the chains of the past. At this point, we are ready to move forward on our journey with love in our hearts instead of hate. Our Beloved is **LOVE**, so anytime we act lovingly, we are grounded in our true self, and when we act unloving, we act from our false self. Love brings peace, while the lack of love brings turmoil.

Love's power enables us to take responsibility for our actions, learn from our mistakes, make amends, and maintain our self-respect. Do you realize how healthy this is? I could never have had the wisdom to do this prior to my experience. I'll quote the Biblical passage, which speaks most eloquently for me on this matter. *"You shall know the Truth, and the Truth will set you free."* (John 8:32) The power of love frees us to live from our true nature.

I began to understand that living in this Transcendent Reality means living with a new set of rules. Our false selves no longer govern us. We no longer thirst after fulfilling our ego needs as we do while inhabiting our physical bodies on earth. In this spiritual reality, where we become **aware** of our perfection in union with our Creator, absolutely everything is seen through the eyes of unconditional love. What matters above all in every single circumstance in a person's earthly life is learning to respond from our core Divinity within. Failure to learn this results in fear and chaos while responding from our true selves results in peace.

During my life review with the Light, I was flabbergasted to understand that even the **simplest** act of kindness that one would overlook as insignificant was a **major act** of our spiritual selves. Our Holiness and perfection despite our human faults appears during those moments when we forget ourselves, and whenever we place the needs of others before our own. That is why those small acts of kindness are so momentous. We think they are so insignificant that we tend not to remember them. But that is precisely when we are at our spiritually best selves. When our ego has no awareness for the need to act lovingly but instead, spontaneously *reacts* lovingly, we are living Holy lives.

It boils down to this. Every moment of every day while we exist on earth, we are given two choices, to react either from a loving or unloving way. Our purpose on earth is to **learn** this lesson. We should never underestimate the significance or size of any situation that enables us to attain this infinite goal. By releasing our heart's feeling, we are releasing the power of our Divine kinship to dispel the spiritual darkness of others wherever we go. Nothing is more important than following the inner Voice of conscience, which is the Voice of our Beloved, and conducting our lives to honor who we are.

As the experience continued, I wanted to remain with the Light forever. I was "home" where I truly belonged. I couldn't bear the thought of being separated from this Holy existence with my Beloved. Consciously, I began to consider a way to do it. I knew that I had to be free of that physical form, that part of me that was delivering the eulogy, so I briefly considered having a heart attack to gain that release. My desire to stay with the Light surpassed any desire I had to live on earth. I have a wonderful loving family whom I love very, very much! Life has been very good to me, so my considerations weren't because of any depression or anything like that. Try to understand, there is absolutely **nothing** on earth that is more important than being "home" with the Light and our Beloved's Love - **NOTHING!**

Knowing my thoughts, the Light communicated telepathically to me the words, *"No, you cannot stay. I have work for you on earth. You are to become a communicator, to help people understand that there is life after death. Help them become aware of their true nature, and help them to learn to live their lives expressing unconditional love for one another."*

My heart was racing with excitement and readiness to accept this work for the Light, but I was told that before I made my decision, I must know what to expect. In a flash forward scene, I was shown the negative aspects of the work I was being called to do. I saw myself standing before audiences speaking of what I had experienced with the Light. People were ridiculing me, laughing, shaking their heads in disbelief, and walking out of my presentations. I saw my entire circle of friends no longer wanting to be friends with me because they felt I was no longer the person I was before, and many thought I had gone crazy. My own family would not believe that I was in the presence of the Creator during a transcendent experience. When I saw all those scenes, I felt very sad. I wasn't sad because people thought I was crazy or fanatical. I was sad for the Creator. People did not want to believe *the message that came from the Light*. I was not interested in calling attention to myself. The ego must not be center stage when one is called to serve. I was sad because I knew how much the Light loved **everyone as much as the Light loved me during my experience. The Light wanted everyone to know about that love through the message that I was being sent back to deliver, and they chose to turn away.** I can't begin to tell you how sad I felt for the Light of God.

In another flash forward scene, I was shown the positive aspects of the work the Light was calling me to do. Once again, I saw myself giving presentations to audiences, and this time they were listening intently, deeply touched by my sincerity. I saw little red hearts being lifted from their bodies upwards toward the Creator's heart for intimacy and renewal. Human consciousness was becoming more elevated to Divine consciousness and self-realization.

To tell you the truth, both scenes did not influence me in making my decision about the "mission" the Light was calling me to do. My mind was already made up the moment the Light asked of me. With passion deep in my soul, I wanted to serve the Light in whatever way I was being called. To use my life in this way was my gift I could give to our Creator in gratitude for the blessed gift the Creator had just given me. Oh yes, I would accept this "calling" no matter what obstacles I had to face along the journey.

When I gave my answer of acceptance, I immediately felt a tremendous infusion of knowledge as if volumes and volumes of material entered my consciousness. I have noticed that this knowledge surfaces only when I am engaged in the actual work for the Light such as writing this book, giving talks, or working with individuals. I am always amazed that this wisdom surfaces because it is not something I have previously read about in someone else's works. When I do come across the material "after the fact," I feel so humbled that my Beloved is helping me with my "calling." I make it a practice not to attend workshops, lectures, or read material set forth by others. It is my way of staying a clear and open channel to the Light. If I didn't hear or read the material beforehand, then when it does surface during my own work, I know that the wisdom came directly from my encounter with the Light. I can be confident that I am being called to share the Light's message, and not man's.

Shortly before the conclusion of my encounter with the Light, this message was telepathically communicated to me:

"With the gift you have now received, go forth and tell the masses that life after death exists. You shall all experience my

profound LOVE! (That word was emphasized as the word I was to promulgate in my work.) *LOVE is the key to the universe. You must all learn to live in peace and harmony with one another on earth while you have the chance. This will be a very difficult task for you my child, but you shall do it. You are **LOVED!***

Confidence in my ability to fulfill the directive came when the Light said, *"As long as you hold onto my hand and don't let go, I shall lead, and you shall follow. I will prepare the way ahead for you."*

What happened next was something remarkable. A scene appeared before me in which I was standing at the head of a very long thick oak wooden table. Seated around the table were twelve individuals who were all dressed in apparel reminiscent of a time period where men wore robe-like garments like the Monks wore. All except the three seated on my right next to me had their robe hoods pulled over their heads, so I could not see their faces. The three men seated next to me had their faces exposed to me. I became aware as I stood before all of them that I was being called to a life of service to humanity, and the twelve individuals were going to be instrumental in helping me to accomplish my earthly mission for the Light.

Deeply humbled for this assistance, I thanked the Light for the part these twelve individuals would serve when I returned once more to the physical realm. These wonderful souls who committed their lives to helping me fulfill my calling for the Light cannot be thanked enough. Although three individuals were revealed to me, and the others were veiled, my prayer for all of them has always been that our Beloved will bless them in some way to show my appreciation for the loving support they have given to help me. It is said that "no man is an island," and I believe that we were created to need one another. When we commit to help one another, we are expressing the Divine Light within us to bring love and Truth onto the earth.

A few years following my experience, the three men seated to my right whose faces were revealed to me came into my life. When I met them, I immediately recognized them from my experience, and I was flabbergasted because they were complete strangers up until then. I did not tell them that they were participating in my experience because I did not want them to feel pressured to help me in any way in my earthly mission. I would leave it up to them to contribute their parts if that was their intended purpose. Their souls would know what to do without their egos getting in the way.

As it turned out, the three men have played a huge role in helping me, and it was only recently that I decided to tell them what part they have played in my life. As for the others seated at the table, I do not know who they are. But I am certain they are the angels that the Light is bringing me to fulfill my earthly mission. I am sure that I will recognize them in the afterlife, and I will have huge hugs for them all!

CHAPTER 9

WHY ME?

Bear witness to me so that awareness of me expands into the hearts of men and women everywhere.

Following my transcendent experience, I asked myself the same question again and again. "Why me?" I couldn't imagine the Light had chosen the right person to carry out this important work. I felt I was lacking so many abilities that were necessary for the work. I wasn't a theologian or someone with a Ph.D. behind my name giving me the intellectual credibility to empower my work. I was just an ordinary woman with a husband, children, and a career. I had an ordinary life like most people.

"Why me?" Over and over again, the question surfaced when I began to be overwhelmed at the thought of the work ahead of me. I was told by the Light that I was to become a communicator and to tell the masses that there is life after death and to bring a message of hope and love to my fellow man. Surely, I thought, the Light made a mistake of judgment. After all, if I were choosing someone, I certainly would not have chosen me. I'm rather a shy person about God and religion. It's such a private, personal matter. I'm not the kind of person who would suddenly start standing on street corners thumping a Bible and preaching salvation. How in the world was I supposed to become a communicator as I was instructed? How was I supposed to write a book? I don't know how to write anything of significance. I would have chosen a much better person who already had a respectable following, a religious leader, or some other well-known person, but me? How would I do it? I had no idea. The only thought I did know was that I wanted passionately to fulfill this work for the Light.

Not only was I dealing with that concern following my experience, but I also had a need to find out whether anyone else in the world had experienced what I did. I knew absolutely and without a doubt that it was an authentic, **REAL** encounter with our Creator, but I also knew that it transcended our ordinary physical sense of reality. Was there anyone in historical biblical times that encountered *light* as a Divine Presence? Was there anyone else in modern day? These questions became a motivating force deep within my heart to find answers to those questions. But how would I find the answers?

Reviewing the experience over in my mind, I began searching for possible means of obtaining this information. Since this experience was not a sensory, physical reality event, I immediately considered the paranormal literature. Surely the library would be a good information source. Searching through stacks of periodicals, I wasn't finding what I was looking for. First of all, I didn't have a name for my experience, so I wasn't sure what I was searching for. I gave up the search in the libraries after weeks of futile attempts.

Since my encounter with the Light dealt with consciousness in a new way, I thought I could contact someone who specializes in the mind, a psychologist or psychiatrist. I immediately canceled that thought. No, he or she would spend all their time trying to convince me that I had a hallucination or delusion, and I would spend all my time denying it and trying to convince them that it was a **REAL** event. I dismissed that idea quickly and moved on to another idea.

Since my experience dealt with the Creator, I would talk with the experts in the field of religion. Of course! Why didn't I think of that in the first place? To avoid getting only one interpretation of my experience, I contacted several clergy covering several of the major religions: Protestant, Catholic, Baptist, and Jewish. I made appointments to speak privately with them fully expecting one of them to provide me with the answers to my questions. I was very anxious to know if anyone from historical biblical times had experienced anything similar to what I did. Since I have not read the Bible, I believed these clergymen were present day Biblical authorities who could enlighten me.

The reception I received from all the clergy was the same. They patiently listened to my account and very politely ushered me out the door. Not one mentioned to me that there was a man named Paul in the Bible whose Light experience on the road to Damascus changed him in much the same way I had been instantly changed. No one ever mentioned that the word "light" was often found written throughout the Bible.

One Baptist minister however, did have some suggestions for me. He said, "You must never talk about this experience to anyone again. Your experience is the work of the devil. There is a passage in the Bible that says Satan can be disguised as an "angel of light." His manner toward me was quite judgmental, and I responded by saying, "How can my experience be the work of Satan? My entire life changed instantly. I have developed such an intimate loving bond with our Creator. I've become so loving and forgiving of others. The passion in my heart is that my life will be used for good in the service of our Creator and my fellow man?" I continued speaking, "Truly, I believe that if my encounter with our Creator was the work of Satan, then wouldn't Satan do everything in his power to lead me **away** from our Creator and prevent me from using my life to glorify the One most High? My experience brought me **to our Creator**, and I fully intend to stay dedicated to our Creator through the work

I was called to do." The minister had no answer to my reply. He merely continued to preach how bad my experience was and how I must not be deceived by Satan working in me. As he led me out the door he said quite angrily that he would pray for me and for my salvation.

I was devastated! With my whole heart I had expected to be supported by the clergy, not rejected. I found it hard to accept that those who propose to know the Creator as messengers of the Holy One couldn't believe that our Creator could perform such a miracle as what was done for me. It got down to a very basic issue for me. If our Creator is both omnipresent and omniscient, it must mean that our Creator has the power to do whatever our Creator chooses to do. It means that if our Creator wanted me, or anyone else for that matter, to hear a Holy Voice and receive a miraculous experiential communion with the Creator, our Beloved can! Jesus did it with Paul on the road to Damascus in early Biblical days, so why can't our Creator do it in modern days? Our Beloved can do **all things**, not just up to a certain limit as the clergy with whom I spoke seemed to think. Their disbelief pierced my heart. What does it say about their faith I wondered?

On the other hand, I tried to understand their viewpoint. If someone came to me and told me they encountered the Creator, I probably would have disbelieved them. As human beings, a spiritual phenomenon is not something one is comfortable hearing because it is not within the framework of everyday experience. My hunch is however, that there are many ordinary people living ordinary lives that have been blessed by a Heavenly Presence, and whose lives have also been spiritually transformed. To step forward and acknowledge that they too, encountered our Creator without being close to death in any way is very intimidating, if not downright scary. Who wants to be judged and labeled eccentric in some way? It's safer to remain quiet and hold the experience close to one's own heart. But it is only by stepping forward and bravely telling humanity that the Creator's Voice is indeed, being heard and that this Divine Voice can spiritually transform our world consciousness if we listen to it!

Talking about my encounter with the Light, my family and friends resulted in bewildered stares and apprehensive attitudes toward me. What so-called "expert" do I contact now to find out if others shared a similar experience? No one, I thought. I had exhausted all hope for an answer and felt heart-broken. I felt so alone as if I were the only one in the world who had this experience. I thought about my near-death experience during childbirth when I died, and I knew that I had encountered the same Light during both my transcendent experiences. I had a desperate need to know if others experienced what I did.

Finally, one morning in my kitchen, I let all my frustrations out as I prayed to my Beloved. The burning question arose once again, "Why me? Why did you choose me to do this work for you?" Over and over again I kept asking, "Why me, why me? Why did you call me to do this work and then fill my heart with so much passion to serve you when I don't know what to do? I am just a simple woman. I feel so unprepared to begin this "calling" you want me to do. Why did you choose me?" I sobbed from the depth of my heart.

When I was emotionally drained, I suddenly began to feel the same energy I experienced fifteen minutes before delivering the eulogy. The energy moved throughout my body in the same manner, first from the toes, then upward along my spine and exiting out the top of my head. Once again, I felt such tremendous, unearthly peace, *the peace that passeth all understanding.* Telepathically, I heard the words, *"Because I chose you my child."*

When I heard those words being conveyed to me with an outpouring of love filling my entire body, the question, "Why me?" was forever erased from my mind. It seemed as if the question no longer was important to me. My need for the answer simply vanished into thin air. *"Because I chose you, my child."* That was my simple, yet truthful answer. Years later, I discovered a passage in the Bible which addresses my question, "Why me?" and it confirms what I heard the Light's Voice saying to me that day. It is from John 15:16. *"Ye did not choose me, but I chose you, and appointed you, that ye should go and bear fruit."* Awesome isn't it?

Several days following my conversation with my Beloved while kneeling on my kitchen floor, I happened to read a very small announcement in our local newspaper under the church news section. Normally, I was not in the habit of reading church news since I didn't belong to a church at the time. It had been only months since my experience, and I had not made any decisions concerning any church involvement. However, something led my eyes to read that announcement, and I believe in retrospect, it was Spirit within that guided me to it. I read that as part of the adult Christian education Lenten series, the church was going to present a book review by Raymond Moody, M.D. called *Life After Life*. Something deeply resonated within the depth of my heart that I must attend the meeting even though I never heard of this book or Raymond Moody, M.D. What was this urgent feeling within me all about? I knew I had to go and find out.

The evening of the meeting, I took my place at the long wooden conference table. Seated, were eight members of the church, all strangers except two. The minister sat at the head of the table to preside over the meeting, and when everyone was ready, he told us to open Dr. Moody's book to search for ideas to generate discussion. Browsing a few pages, I was immediately pulled into the story like a strong magnet. It was as if the words were jumping out at me. Oh my goodness, this is incredible, I thought. Someone else in this book is describing exactly what I experienced! They were using words to describe their own experience with the Light and with the same feelings I had about my own, like "ineffable," meaning there are no words to describe the experience, because it goes beyond words.

This was the first time that I became aware that I was not alone. Others experienced what I did. The only difference was that they were all near-death at the time. I wasn't. I was delivering a eulogy at the time. It didn't matter to me that the preliminary event leading up to the actual experience was different. What mattered was the *experience itself!* We were all describing the same spiritual event that transformed our lives. Excitedly, I blurted out to the group, "This is exactly what happened to me!" Michael, the minister, continued asking me further questions about my experience. To my astonishment, he was accepting everything I told him with such openness. I could sense he was exuding unconditional love toward me. He wasn't judging my experience or me like all the other clergy who I had met did. A wonderful healing took place for me that evening. My need to know if any others had ever had the kind of experience I had and whether there was any precedence for the experience recorded in the Bible was answered.

Michael began telling me about a man named Paul in the Bible. Paul, a Jew, was the leading persecutor of Christians. About five years after the crucifixion of Jesus, Paul was on his way to Damascus when a brilliant Light from Heaven surrounded him and instantly changed his life. From 2 Corinthians 12:2-4, *"I know a certain Christian man who fourteen years ago was snatched up to the highest heaven...and there he heard things which cannot be put into words, things that human lips may not speak."* When Paul was asked by the voice in his vision, *Saul, Saul!* (Paul's given Jewish name), *"Why do you persecute me?"* Paul could only ask in return, *"Who are you, Lord?"* The voice answered, *"I am Jesus, whom you persecute."* (Acts 9:4-5) From that moment on, Paul knew the vision was real, and that Jesus was speaking to him in a vision (Acts 26:9). Immediately he began to proclaim his faith in Jesus and began teaching that the Messiah's message was not only for Jews but also for Gentiles. Paul became the most influential voice throughout the history of Christianity, except for Jesus Himself.

Michael taught me some things about Paul that I did not know and of which I personally identified. The first characteristic both Paul and I experienced as a result of our transcendent encounter with the Holy One was humility, feeling the "least," not smarter or greater than anyone else. The second characteristic we both experienced was the feeling of being completely unworthy of Divine mercy and grace. Another similarity in both our experiences was that Divine Grace illumined our spirits, and we were instantly transformed causing a passionate dedicated calling from our Creator to share the Divine message of love for everyone. Now that's a miracle!

Driving home from the church meeting that evening, tears once more streamed down from my eyes as I thanked my Beloved for answering my need to know that there were indeed others who shared my experiential encounter with the Light. Feeling jubilant with this knowledge, I knew that my Beloved was mysteriously bringing me what I needed. Not only did I learn that individuals who were near-death shared this profound experience with me, but the minister's unconditional acceptance of me and my experience proved to be a turning point for me. I decided that evening that I would work to provide experiencers with that same kind of support. I would give back to others in some way, the kind of healing strength I had just received that evening.

In 1981, the International Association of Near-Death studies, Inc. was formed (IANDS). A non-profit organization, it is the only organization in the world whose mission it is to respond to "people's needs for information and support concerning near-death and near-death-like experiences and to encourage recognition of the experiences as genuine and significant events of rich meaning." I became a member and quickly decided that

I could fulfill the promise to provide other near-death experiencers with the kind of support I had been given. If you want more information about this wonderful organization, contact them at: IANDS, 2741 Campus Walk Ave. Bldg. 500, Durham, NC 27705-8878 or their website at www.iands.org.

In 1984, I founded the Columbus, Ohio IANDS organization. To this day, I continue to serve as its coordinator. Our informal meetings offer needed support to individuals who have had near-death, near-death-like and similar transformative experiences. Reliable research information is also discussed in order to offer an educational approach as well. Interested health care workers, clergy, families, and friends of experiencers, and interested members of the general public constitute our membership. For information about the Columbus, Ohio IANDS organization, please check their website: **www.freewebs.com/iandsolumbus**.

At this time, I would like to draw attention to the confusion of the general population between the near-death experience and the near-death-like experience. You will see similarities between them. The differences are the triggers that precipitate the experience. The way we came to the Light is unimportant. Some people are near-death, others may have non-trauma triggers, such as delivering a eulogy, meditating, resting, or simply going about their daily lives. These spiritually transcendent experiences are really **mystical experiences** and the confusion began when Raymond Moody, M.D. coined a spin-off term to focus only on one particular trigger releaser - coming close to death. But the reality is that there are many different triggers all resulting in what should be called, mystical experiences. Whatever the trigger, these experiences are the same. The events leading up to the actual experience are not part of the actual experience itself for <u>the "experience" BEGINS once consciousness transcends the physical body and enters into a different dimension other than the physical dimension. This transcendent experience ends once consciousness returns to the physical body.</u> I cannot emphasize this enough for there is growing confusion about these very similar experiences and in what category to place very similar experiences. I wish Dr. Moody would have simply called it like it really is - a mystical experience which comprises all transcendent experiences regardless whether one is close to death or not.

To illustrate what I am trying to say, I am going to list the characteristics of a near-death experience and their aftereffects. As you recall from my own experience during the time that I was speaking the eulogy, you can see that *I experienced the identical features of a classic near-death experience without coming close to death, suffering serious illness or physical trauma.*

ELEMENTS OF A CLASSIC NEAR-DEATH EXPERIENCE THAT I ALSO EXPERIENCED DURING MY NEAR-DEATH-LIKE EXPERIENCE:

- Out of body
- Unearthly peace
- Dark void
- Traveling at fast rate of speed
- Being with deceased loved ones
- Encountering a Being of Light
- Life review
- Life preview
- Unconditional love
- Total knowledge
- Being told "it's not your time; you have to return"
- Rapidly returning to physical consciousness
- A sense of mission or calling

TYPICAL AFTEREFFECTS

- Loss of the fear of death
- Becoming more spiritually orientated transcending divisiveness of religious sectarianism
- Appreciation for the beauty of life
- Love and concern for others
- Loss of interest in materialism
- Increase in psychic development
- Charismatic personality
- Increased intelligence
- Latent talents and creativity surface

As you can see from the above list, I had the identical elements of a classic near-death experience while I was delivering a eulogy. Can you now see how confusing the term near-death experience can be when you have someone like me experiencing the same elements of a near-death experience, but who wasn't close to death at the time?

In 1992, the International Association for Near-Death Studies, Inc. researched the phenomenon of near-death experiences by sending out a questionnaire to which 229 individuals replied. Twenty-three percent of the respondents had their experience during clinical death, forty percent during a serious illness or physical trauma, and thirty-seven percent had an experience without trauma or serious illness of any kind. This legitimate research by the world's foremost organization dedicated to the study of death and dying has confirmed what so many within our population have experienced - transformation of consciousness. You can see that the *lowest* percentage of individuals having this experience occurred during clinical death, and the highest percentage belonging to the group who experienced serious illness or physical trauma. However, you can also see that the group that shared almost the same percentage were the individuals who were not close to death, suffered serious illness or physical trauma. These statistics speak volumes about the fact that one does not have to be close to death, illness, or trauma to have the same experience as someone who was.

To further illustrate my point regarding the unimportance of the trigger mechanism that initiates transcendent consciousness, let's say a large mountain is in front of us, beckoning our desire to reach the top. Some people will use a car, another intends to walk, another uses a helicopter, another takes the path that twists and turns, and another takes the path that is straight. Can you see that all the travelers will reach the top, albeit different ways or triggers? Each will have a different account of how they arrived at the summit based upon their method of travel. Yes, it will be fascinating to learn of the details of their trip up the mountain, but once they arrive at the destination at the summit, each person will have the same view of the horizon.

The same is true of experiences that bring us to the Light. No person's personal journey to the Light is more credible or more important than anyone else's journey. True mystical experiences such as near-death and near-death-like experiences as well as other spiritually transformative experiences result in a lasting transformation of an individual that results in feelings of gratitude, renewal, inner peace, and a genuine outpouring of love and compassion for the children of the earth. So whatever path one takes on his/her journey toward the Light, the manifesting behavior results in a call to help others, a sincere innate yearning to help bring about peace and harmony in the world. We should listen to everyone who has heard His Voice through these transcendent mystical transformative experiences for each has been granted a gift of Grace to share with us.

CHAPTER 10

AFTEREFFECTS

The experience of the mysterious Will within oneself is that part of the Divine that ebbs through us performing Divine work in us.

My encounter with the Light radically changed my values, habits, aims, and purposes. In one split second, I was no longer a woman whose life was dominated by a past of fear, guilt, and a belief that God did not love me. **I KNEW GOD LOVED ME!** Knowledge replaced belief. I was brand new; I felt energized and ready and willing to face a future secure in the knowledge that what I had just experienced was **real and truthful**. No one could ever take that truth away from me! The Light had just miraculously transformed my entire being. It was the most precious, sacred, and humbling event in my entire existence. It would be up to me now to either accept it and integrate it into my daily life or reject it when the world's ways put the pressure on me. I chose to honor the gift by sharing that gift with others no matter what the cost to me personally. Let others scoff or ridicule me. My promise to the Light to communicate unconditional love **for all of us** is what resides in the deepest part of my heart and soul. I will not forsake the promise I made to the Light the day I was in the bosom of Divine Light and Divine Love.

The most momentous change that took place within me is my relationship with my Beloved, who is the center of my life now. Everything else is secondary. There is no power in the entire universe that will ever draw me away from my Beloved again. The Divine Presence residing within me and in everything I see, continually nourishes my spiritual self. I hunger and thirst for the Divine, not out of any sense of deprivation, but out of love for the One who loves us beyond comprehension. I become intoxicated, hopelessly longing within for more and more of the intimacy with the Source of my being. My speech cannot be contained when I think of my Beloved. Whether I am talking to a friend, a stranger, an audience, a flower, a bird, or to myself, my words will eventually spill forward to glorify the One who gave me new life. The greatest joy in my life comes when I speak of the Light and the unconditional love that is meant **for all of us no matter what we did or failed to do.**

Today, a fire of passion burns deep within me to carry out my "calling" with the same commitment I had when my near-death-like experience occurred on January 29, 1979. That length of time speaks of the tremendous impact and change that took place within my heart and soul to serve the Divine above all else until I draw my final breath. It would have been much simpler just to have had the encounter with the Light and afterward, sit back and bask in the memory of the bliss. Certainly, it would have been much easier to not discuss it with others and save myself a lot of frustration in being thought of as crazy or fanatical. But I can't do that. My love for our Creator surpasses my ego's desire to remain quiet. When my Great Teacher gave me the understanding of the spiritual aspects of human life, my innermost moral fiber has remained steadfast through all my joys and sorrows. This Spirit within me is where I derive my all-pervading strength to resist the labels or any criticism I may face while serving my life's higher purpose. I hear my Beloved's Voice in the assurance of the Holy Presence within encouraging me to love and help others. This is what I was called to do, and I will not transgress from that directive.

I never push anyone beyond what they are willing to accept. I simply share what I have learned and allow others to make their own decisions. If they have eyes, they will see. If they have ears, they will hear. I merely encourage them to open their minds a crack, and when they do, I believe they have given themselves an opportunity to hear our Creator's Voice more intimately in their own personal, spiritual lives. Life brings more joy to those who hear Spirit's Voice.

The Light lives inside my heart right now as love. If you could hear my heartbeat, you would hear the sound of joy singing its transcendent song of love sweeping throughout all the cells of my body. Love, joy, and peace are the gifts that have remained a part of me since 1979. In the midst of losing all my posses-sions when our house burned in 1988, the death of my beloved parents, family illness, pressures of daily living, I have been able to meet life's challenges with love, joy, and peace intact deep within me. My whole mind and heart changed that blissful day. I can honestly say, to be one with God renews our very being so that our interior and exterior life is a reflection of our true, loving selves. In the deepest sense, my life is nurtured by a deeper affinity of love, compassion, kindness, and service to humanity.

There have been other changes in me that have continued to remain with me to this day. No longer do I feel attachment toward materialism. I appreciate what I do have and view them as blessings, but I no longer want to impress others with my belongings. When we lost all of our possessions during our house fire, I didn't grieve over anything. They are objects; they can be replaced. My family escaped unharmed amidst the fiery rage of flames. We all survived, and that is what is important.

From a human standpoint, it can be easy to despair when we are enveloped in a myriad of nasty events. Our outer-world is filled with fear and chaos rendering us weak and powerless to overcome our adversities. I have learned however, that the Light's all-pervading Love is ceaselessly infusing within us, the strength to sustain us even when we are not aware of it.

Before my encounter with the Light, I had no self-esteem, a perfectionist, judgmental, unforgiving, and a host of other negative qualities. But *immediately* following my return back from my near-death-like experience, those qualities disappeared. I became very loving toward God, self, and others, not in the old way that says if you are nice to me, I'll be nice to you. Instead, my actions speak more of unconditional love, the love that says I love you, no strings attached. One is already worthy simply by being a part of the Divine at the core of our being and revealing a conviction that all people are of one Divine Essence.

It is however, difficult for me to embrace *unloving behavior* in others. That kind of behavior that dishonors the very root of our being continually rips my heart in shreds. Wrongdoing should always be confronted. Un-confronted, the wrongful behavior encourages an individual to continue that behavior. Therefore, it is one of the most compassionate things you can do for someone to help heal their wrongdoing. One day when they shall return "home" to live in the spiritual realm, they will have their life review during which time they will clearly understand their relationship to our Creator. It is during this life review that they will realize every single moment of their lives that they displayed behavior that was not inherent in their spiritually rooted identity.

No one escapes this life review process of self-discovery. It can be a very unpleasant experience to those who have displayed unloving behavior when they instantaneously comprehend the meaning and purpose of their life - *"love one another, just as I love you."* Unlike our physical consciousness, which we often disregard if we want to, our spiritual consciousness becomes **actualized** at that point, and we **become** Truth itself. Our comprehension of all matters is so clearly understood and unmistakably free from errors or false perceptions that it is **impossible** to dismiss the discernment of that truth.

It is with this direct knowledge from my own experience that I am able to understand others unloving behavior in a much deeper and compassionate way than I had previously. Inwardly, however, I still yearn for that individual to "wake up and see the Light" before that time comes when their self-realization becomes apparent in the spiritual dimension. *Earthly life has been given to us to learn how to love!* This is the message that was so infused into my consciousness when I was united in love with my Great Teacher. Every moment is an opportunity to learn that lesson.

Crossing over to the spiritual dimension illuminates one's soul of that purpose on earth. That is when the soul discovers that knowledge and is jolted into the full realization of that truth. It is like a light bulb turning on in your brain. "So that's what it's all about," I recall thinking while I was before my Great Teacher. This profound wisdom is shared with you in the hope that you will choose to live lovingly while you have the many opportunities that appear before you. Every one of us should prepare ourselves for the afterlife by directing our attention to our thoughts and actions beginning at this very moment. It is imperative that we resolve our differences and misunderstandings with one another. If no one cares enough to do so, then our earthly lives can never be lived in peace and harmony. Perhaps listening to the vast numbers of individuals who have encountered the Divine down through the ages, saints, mystics, and sages of all religions, near-death experiencers, near-death-like experiencers, and others who have had spiritually transformative experiences, humanity can begin to comprehend the one message that echoes throughout the voices of all those experiencers - **LOVE ONE ANOTHER!**

There have been other noticeable changes within me

following my encounter with the Light. The perfectionism in me has subsided. I still put forth my best effort, but I no longer feel my sense of worth is tied into it if I succeed or fail. Seeing the sacred in all things was definitely a beautiful change that took place deep within my heart. I became aware that all life forms are sacred and are a part of the Divine. From the smallest ant to the tallest tree, I feel so connected to the life-force that flows through everything. Every single life form that inhabits our world is part of the Divine Mysterious Presence with us, and with reverence, I feel especially grateful for that enhanced awareness of the Divine in all things. Remember I mentioned that the Light showed me that everything has at the core of its being, Divine Light.

I feel closest to my Beloved in nature, and I spend many hours in quiet solitude seated on an old oaken log in the woods where I live, communing with Spirit. I am continually nurtured when the cool gentle breeze playfully dances with my short brown hair, and the warm sunlight, filtering through the tall ash trees, softly touches my hazel eyes. Spirit's Voice is heard among the sweet songbirds passing overhead to let me know that all is well. Nature's solitude refreshes my soul as water quenches my thirst.

The bond I feel with animals is very, very strong. My heart swells with love that is so simple and pure, asking nothing in return but the opportunity to participate in the Holy life that our Creator has provided for us. There have been occasions when wild animals have rested at my feet when I am communing with Spirit in nature's world. One day a raccoon appeared, and as I was talking to it, it came closer to me and unafraid of me, proceeded to climb up my back and took a short nap on my shoulders. The visits that I have with my animal friends are moments of sheer bliss!

I am reminded of the time my family and I went to a picnic on a 175-acre farm. While mingling with others, I noticed a fawn in the distance. I told my husband I was going to visit the fawn for a while. He chuckled at my loving sensitivity for animals and understood that my love for them runs very deep. Dean smiled at the child-like sparkle in my eyes as I wandered off toward the fawn.

As I slowly approached her, I couldn't help but notice how beautiful she was. She was an exquisite creation from our Creator and how breathtaking she was standing before me. Her eyes glistened with Light, and she looked at me with a penetrating gaze that told me she was not afraid of me. My own eyes transmitted back to her, the instinctive tender love I felt for her. She must have sensed the extraordinary love emanating from me to her because she did not back away or act startled in any way.

I sat down on the damp moss under a large oak tree and kept talking softly to her. She came toward me and to my delight, lying down beside me, she put her head on my knees. Stroking her velvety head, I kept talking to her in a soft, gentle manner, and we bonded in a way that no words can convey. She felt safe, contented, and loved. With her head cradled in my arms, she began to lick the salt from my arms with her warm soft tongue. I felt so blessed by the Divine Presence, whose love was tenderly saturating me in the middle of the tall oak trees at the edge of the forest. His Voice could be heard in the silent intimacy of my heart revealing to me, the reality of Oneness.

A half hour had passed so quickly, and I knew I had to return to the others at the picnic. Softly I said, "I have to leave now." At that precise moment, the fawn began to emit a shrill sound that could only be interpreted as a distress cry. I had not yet moved in any way to alert her that I was about to get up. Somehow she knew that I was going to leave her because she kept crying and making a whimpering sound that pierced my heart. I ached for her and longed to remain with her but knew the time had come for our separation.

Suddenly, she stood up and firmly placed her leg over mine in what appeared to be an attempt to say, "Don't go!" Over and over again, her leg motioned me to stay on the ground with her. I have absolutely no doubt that we were communicating with one another through the language of unconditional love, a language that comes directly from Spirit and knows no boundaries. Tears streamed down from my eyes as I stood up and tenderly kissed her head and said goodbye.

When I returned to the picnic, I asked the hostess about the fawn. She told me days earlier, the fawn's mother had been killed on the road and the fawn was alone. She was probably no older than six weeks. It became apparent to me that every single time we give our love away, not only does that love find its union with another, but love miraculously returns full circle to us. The special moments I share with nature are moments of pure ecstasy and union with the Divine experienced in all.

Prior to my encounter with the Light, I was like most people who drive their cars and see dead remains of animals along the road. I noticed they were there but only as debris, which should be avoided so as not to get the car's tires dirty. I never gave the animal much thought. But it is a different story since my encounter with the One who creates all life. I stop to consider that the animal may have shared a nurturing, loving bond within its own family unit. I ask myself if it left behind young orphans to fend for themselves. In a very deep and intimate sense, I feel connected to the animal that God created and feel a sense of loss for that life.

My heart is prompted to say a prayer for every dead animal I see alongside the road. "I pray for you precious one. May you be in Heaven with our Heavenly Father and may I see you in Heaven one day. God loves you and so do I." My eyesight is failing and there have been times when I've said prayers for remnants of tires or other debris mistaking it for a dead animal. When that happens, I chuckle first, and then reverently, offer the prayer up for another animal whose life was taken in some way. Prayers when spoken from the heart are never wasted. *All life is sacred!*

Another change that took place within me is the fear of death. No longer do I fear it. I am afraid of the dying process because like most people, I detest pain and suffering. But to die, oh no, there is absolutely no fear at all. In fact, I am looking forward to that beautiful day when I am once again reunited with my Beloved. It is a homecoming that I cherish with all my heart and soul. But let me also say, I do not want to check out of this life before my time, at least not until my life's work for the Light has been completed. Serving the One who blessed me so much is my ultimate purpose on this earth. When I finally do go back "home," I want to be able to say that I gave it "my best shot."

Death should be thought of as a beautiful experience rather than the dreaded event that we have been conditioned to think. Unfortunately, most of us view death through the eyes of fear. Fear of the unknown is downright scary for many of us. There are, however, many people who have had near-death experiences who return to waking consciousness to tell us what it is like to die. Again and again a common thread is woven throughout these experiences. Death is not what we think it is; it is a very beautiful, wonderful revelation of remarkable intensity. The Light of God is steadfast and does not change so the feeling of being "home" again is felt no matter what path leads you there. It doesn't matter if you went "home" to be with the Light through a near-death, a near-death-like experience, a mystical or any other trigger releaser. Once you have encountered the Light, that knowledge is solidified in the realization of that truth. Although I encountered the Light twice, once during clinical death and the second time during my near-death-like experience, an encounter with the Light is the same yesterday, today, and will be tomorrow. The Light is the Light just as a human being is a human being. No amount of intellectualism can change that.

Many years have passed since my 1979 near-death-like experience. My mother, father, and my soul-mate husband have since died, but I often talked with them about my experience when they were alive. I am at peace knowing that now they know what I experienced with the Divine Light. I am so happy for them! I can cry tears of JOY when I think that they are experiencing what I did. This knowledge has been a huge, huge comfort to me as I moved through my grief process. However, I do miss their human, physical presence with me big time! This is normal; we should miss them and grieve appropriately. But if I had a magical wand to bring them back to me, I would not. How could I deny them the greatest LOVE, PEACE, and JOY that they have ever experienced? There is NOTHING on the face of the earth that is better than being "home" again with the Light of God, not even our own love for them. Our loved ones have graduated from earth school, and their reward has been granted to them upon their arrival "home." I experienced first-hand, the other Heavenly dimension twice. I **KNOW** what my loved ones are experiencing, and I am comforted in knowing that one day we will once again be re-united with them. It is only a temporary separation.

Ever since my encounter with the Light, I have been communicating the message I was given by my Great Teacher to share with others. I speak of the spiritual crisis I went through, believing that God could not love me and the absolute devastation that false belief had upon my life. Just as the flash forward scene that the Light showed me during my experience, hearts are being lifted closer to the Divine in some way when I share my experience and my life so openly and lovingly with others. I am so humbled when I receive emails or conversations with people who tell me what a difference my story made in their lives. That is all that matters - inspiring others toward the transcendent nature of life and loving union with the Divine Presence.

I have given presentations for colleges, universities, professional conferences, churches, hospitals, and community organizations. I have also been interviewed on radio and television. Leading researchers and authors have documented my experiences in their books: *Heading Toward Omega*, and *Lessons From the Light*, by Kenneth Ring, Ph.D.; *After the Beyond*, by Charles P. Flynn, Ph.D.; *Beyond the Light*, and *Near-Death Experiences: The Rest of the Story*, by P.M.H.Atwater; *Spiritual Awakenings*, by Barbara Harris Whitfield, and *Visits From Heaven*, and *Visits To Heaven*, by Josie Varga. I have also been a consultant to many journalists including Jim Auer, who wrote *"Understanding a Near-Death Experience,"* written for Care Notes by Abbey Press.

Certainly it is not for ego's sake that I mention the above work I have accomplished, but rather it is from the deep reverence for my service to my Great Teacher as I promised. *"You will know them by what they do,"* (Matthew 7:16) is perhaps a credible indication of the powerful, transformative nature the experience had upon my life. I have come a long way since those early days when I had no idea how I would carry out the directive the Light gave me. But I must give credit where credit is due. Throughout all these years, Spirit has been right beside me preparing the way ahead for me, just as the Light promised me when I was embraced in the Holy One's Love. The opportunities to communicate the Light's message of love and hope surface before me, and the only thing I do is recognize the opportunity, thank Spirit for bringing it to me, and then I act upon it in order to serve my soul's promise and plan for my life.

The noted research authors I just mentioned are each in their own unique and special way, an instrument of the Light's love to all of us. Their written voices within the pages of their books are truly inspirational as each seeks to honor their higher selves. I am so deeply grateful that the Light prepared the way ahead for me and led me to these remarkable individuals. Each one became a dear, cherished friend of mine, and they are constant reminders to me that the Light's love always works through us to touch others in the most endearing ways.

I have come to the realization that the key to my newfound happiness has been the self-emptying of my ego's will and being receptive to the guidance from the Divine Voice within me. I am then in a position to be of greater service to humanity. Take this book for instance, very early in the writing process I had cut off the source of inspiration by my ego's need to write the book. I learned very quickly that I was in a fog of muddled thinking, and I could not write without tremendous difficulty. When governed by my ego needs, there was no inspiration, and I couldn't write. Realizing that by dwelling on fear thoughts and self-limitations, I had shut off the light switch to my soul consciousness that was ready and able to write the inspired words written in this book. Once I connected to Divine Consciousness through deep prayer and meditation and when I completely trusted the Holy Spirit to bring this book into manifestation, I found the writing, indeed, became inspired and very easy to do. With absolute certainty I can say that my ego self did not write this book. I believe it was my Higher Power or Spirit within that inspired me as I listened intuitively to the Voice within me. The writing in this book surpasses my present abilities to communicate in the style of the beautiful language that it is written. I do not write nor do I speak this way in my ordinary life. Divine Guidance has mysteriously written through the pencil of my hand to bring the message that the Light wants all of us to hear. All glory goes to the Light, the true author of this book.

You must be curious about my feeling regarding the priest who long ago had a great impact upon my spiritual life. I hold no resentment in my heart for him at all. Remember, I said that during my encounter with the Light that there was underlying spiritual good in all the events in our lives, even the most tragic ones. To many, this may sound ludicrous because our ego-based identities cannot discern anything good when confronted with tragic circumstances. Pain usually ensues and robs one of the ability to perceive anything but agonizing bitterness. Beneath the surface of our humanness lies the mystery of our spiritual nature that cannot be comprehended by the limited awareness of the human mind. The best we can do when we suffer is to find meaning in our suffering and that we may fulfill the purpose of our mission. I know this for certain!

The Light of God loves **all of us** not more nor less than anyone else, and is a God who cares. "God loves each of us as if there were only one of us." (Saint Augustine) This is precisely what I experienced! Every person has a unique purpose to fulfill with his or her life. Quietly, Spirit works with us to prepare us for the work that we have to do. All of our life experiences become the necessary training processes that enable us to fulfill our destiny.

I learned during my experience that Spirit participates in our suffering by finding a way to help us go through it and overcome our suffering. Through all the events of our joyous and sorrowful lives, the Holy Comforter is right there with us yearning to have us look up and have the faith that there is a plan for our lives. Only through absolute faith that the Light will not forsake us can we begin to see with greater vision our part in the overall plan for our lives. Those who genuinely seek spiritual understanding and intimacy with the Holy One will receive the guidance and comfort that is needed to fulfill their life's "mission." When we give up our own human self-sufficiency or ego, and find that we cannot solve our problems, instead of looking down in despair, it is time to look up.

One day while picking blackberries, I was inspired to think about the similarity of the blackberry bush and life's difficulties. Standing in front of the eight-foot tall blackberry bush, I saw that it was bursting with plump berries. My senses reeled with exuberant anticipation as I imagined all the delicious jams and pies I would make with them. The juicy berries, warmed by the hot summer sun, were gently placed in my basket, and I was so delighted to see the amount I had collected. However, the amount was not sufficient enough for all that I had hoped. With a determined look, my eyes scanned the bush always searching for more. My vision was limited. I thought, "What if I changed my view and kneeled on the grass and looked up from that perspective?" As I did so, I was delighted to find more of the plump berries hiding under the thick foliage waiting for me to harvest. I had to clear some of the cobwebs that had formed and was pricked several times by the sharp thorns protruding from the stems of the bush, but now my vision affirmed there was more to see. Instead of limiting my vision from the stance I had previously taken, I was in a finer position to continue the process in receiving the abundance of the fruit the bush was providing for me.

Certainly, life will bring us thorns and cobwebs to deal with, and our vision will be limited, but that is precisely the time when we must change our perspective and look up! Our Creator wants to reveal and liberally give us the fruits of the Spirit, but we also should ask. Spirit will not reveal those fruits until we have convinced Spirit that we hold no other desire than to intensely yearn for our Creator with all our heart. When we love our Creator with great passion, our Creator will be revealed to us. We will hear Spirit's Voice deep within our inner being. Remember, our Beloved loves **YOU**.

When I look back upon my own life, my insights are made clear. In my particular journey, the Light had apparently planned to use me as an instrument of Divine Love, which would have a profound spiritual influence upon the lives of others. Looking back upon my life, I can clearly see that my Beloved was grooming me in preparation for the work I am doing now. First came my childhood loving bond with God, which was the result of hearing His Voice that day in the small Ukrainian Church in Hazleton. My modeling career and the numerous beauty pageant titles I won were not mere accidents. Working with photographers and cameras, being interviewed by reporters, public speaking, and publicity appearances, all played a key role in developing my personality traits that unknowingly, would serve a much higher purpose for the Divine later on in my life. That training prepared me to be comfortable when I speak to audiences today.

The apparent "tragedy" in my life occurred when I allowed a priest to be instrumental in shattering my personal relationship with my Beloved. The emotional pain I experienced was horrendous. It affected every aspect of my life. If someone had told me that there was underlying good to be found in that situation, I would have retorted with some cynical response. But I am able to see the underlying **spiritual good** in that so-called tragic situation. In order for me to do my work for the Light of God today as a communicator of Divine **unconditional love for all of us**, it was absolutely necessary for me to experience a situation where I felt so separated from God. Why?

There is no better way to empathize and understand the feelings of others in similar situations than by actually experiencing it oneself. We cannot speak of things we have never experienced. So by sharing my spiritual tragedy with others, I am opening my very soul with them and allowing them to identify and face their own areas of personal crisis with renewed hope. It is somewhat like joining hands and saying, "I've been there, I understand." All too often people feel so unworthy of our Creator's Love that it is hard for them to believe that God would show any interest in them so they distance *themselves* from our Beloved, and their spiritual lives suffer as a result. That is precisely what I did many years ago.

Apparently, our Creator knew a long time ago that in order for me to communicate the Light's message of love and hope for humanity, I had to be able to relate to people and understand their suffering. The priest, therefore, played a necessary role in preparing me to work with Spirit later in my life. I view the priest's involvement in my spiritual crisis as a gift he gave to me because the Holy One was then able to set into motion the rest of the Divine plan to teach me about the unconditional love the Light has for **all of us** despite our faults and weaknesses. After I learned that important lesson during my near-death-like experience with the Light, I would be fully prepared to embark upon my calling to speak to others of the Light's unconditional love for them as well. I was called by the Light to bring that message to everyone who will listen. It is such a simple message that echoes through all the great religions of the world, but it is the stubborn ego in the hearts of so many who refuse to listen to Spirit's Voice within.

When others listen to me speak of the sorrow I endured believing God no longer loved me, many can identify with me. They may not have had the same spiritual crisis as I, but they can identify with the feelings of separation from God, whether it is from fear, guilt, or remorse. So often people are guided by erroneous thoughts and are misled by human will. Obscured by the conflicts of our everyday lives, we lose the inner guidance needed to have renewed faith in a deity who could love us despite what we may have done in the past.

It is possible to learn from the mistakes of others if there is a strong desire to do so, thus saving oneself from an endless search for meaning and ultimate peace. My personal struggle of feeling alienated from God's love and the kind of life that resulted because of that false belief was a sure sign that I had no understanding of my innate spiritual potential. No one could convince me that God could love me even though others tried to change my belief. It took an actual encounter of Divine intervention to instantly erase that ego-determined *perception* and replace it with Divine **Truth**.

The wisdom that was given to me during those precious moments that I spent with the Light of God was meant not only for me personally to heal me of my false belief, but **was meant to be shared with humanity. Everything that my Great Teacher taught me was intended to help others release their own false beliefs so that we could all evolve spiritually toward our Divine-given destiny.**

Love speaks with a depth of innocence that is communicable. Once you have savored the love of the Divine Presence within, you will never want anything else to replace that feeling. The love of God is what we are all craving, and we can have it once we attain deeper spiritual awareness.

Oh my goodness, I marvel at the way Spirit works through every single one of us. Spirit will use us as instruments that we may hear Spirit's Voice to let the world know that there is a God. God's Love heals! If I had to endure spiritual pain and suffering for many years, it was worth it! I emerged from it a changed person forever. I found meaning in my suffering. Along the journey, I have inspired many to open their hearts to the indwelling Presence of the Divine so that they can begin to experience the beauty and mystery of God's personal love for them through the mystical moments that await them. Just as the Light showed me during my experience, hearts are being lifted closer to Divine Consciousness in some way. There is no greater service to the Light and to my fellow man.

One of the aftereffects of my near-death-like experience has been the gift of healing. I am very shy about this aspect for I do not want anyone to believe that I, Nancy Clark, can heal anyone. I do not heal....the Creator does! I am only used as an instrument in the process, and I have no control over who gets healed and who does not. I received this gift about a year or two following my experience. It came about in the following manner. One night I had a dream. I saw white clouds and nothing else. A man's voice called out to me and said, *"Unto you I give the gift of healing."* That was the end of the dream.

When I awoke in the morning, I dismissed the dream because at that time I absolutely did not believe that any human being had the power to heal anyone. I simply turned my back on that dream and went about my daily business. The next night, I had the same dream. Once again upon awakening from the dream, I dismissed it. The following night and each consecutive night

for one full year the same reoccurring dream appeared. I am a slow learner! Finally, one day I prayed and said to God, "If you are actually trying to get my attention in this recurrent dream, and you want me to have the gift of healing (even though I didn't believe in healing), then I will accept the gift. But I will only accept the gift if I know the dream is really and truly coming from you God, and you are calling me to serve you in this way. If I am being called, I don't know how to heal; you will have to show me, and if the dream is not coming from you, then please take this dream away once and for all!"

That night the same dream appeared, the same white clouds and a voice saying, *"Unto you I give the gift of healing."* The dream continued. Suddenly, my younger brother appeared as a seven-year-old with child-like faith, looking into my eyes. He was in need of healing. The voice instructed me to raise the level of my love for my brother to the level I experienced during my encounter with the Holy One during my experience and then to say the words three times, "In Jesus' name, be healed." I did that. Then from out of the clouds came a tremendous thunder-bolt of electrical energy that passed through the top of my head, through my body, and out from my hands into my brother's body. My brother fell over from the energy, and he was healed. The dream ended.

Well, you can imagine how I felt when I woke up from this dream. I felt bewildered, apprehensive, and stunned. This time I knew the dream had been given to me as an added calling, but I didn't know when or on whom I would use that gift.

I needed confirmation. Did I really have this gift? I decided to try my first attempt at healing on my dog. He was old and for the past year his bladder lost all control every time he stood up from a lying position. He was asleep lying on the floor when I approached him. I did exactly as my dream had instructed me to do, and then I nudged my dog to stand up. When he did, his bladder did not lose control and spill urine all over the floor as he had always done. I was shocked because this was the first time in a year that he didn't lose control of his bladder. He was healed of this condition and remained that way for the remainder of his life. That confirmation allowed me to stretch past my shyness a bit to help others if that was what I was called to do. I go about this healing work very quietly and usually do this through prayerful communion with my Beloved. I find for whatever reason, this healing gift works best when I am working with animals instead of humans.

CHAPTER 11

ENHANCED ABILITIES

We don't need to understand the mystery of man's own complex nature in order to embrace our God-given gifts. To use those gifts, however, is entirely our own decision.

Enhanced abilities have become more prevalent in my life following my encounter with my Great Teacher. Strongest perhaps, would be precognitive dreams. This has taken the form of witnessing future events before they happen and after-death communications. After-death communications or "ADCs," a term coined by Bill and Judy Guggenheim in their book, *Hello From Heaven,* is the first complete study of spiritual experiences occurring when a deceased loved one spontaneously and directly contacts someone.

I am so glad to see this kind of serious research taking place for it allows so many people the opportunity to have their own ADC experiences validated and offers comfort and hope to so many people. In sharing a few of my own ADCs with you, it is my hope that it will inspire you to realize that life is truly a continuum and a wondrous marvel of Divine Intent. My intent in writing about these unusual experiences is not to dazzle you with my special enhanced abilities in order to inflate myself in your eyes. While it is true that I consider these abilities "gifts,"

I do not become attached to these powers so that I lose sight of my intended purpose: *to serve thee, not me.* In all things, I try to live my life bringing honor and glory to our Creator. These gifts came from a Higher Power, and they must be used for good - never for selfish or impure motives. In sharing the following accounts with you, I will simply open to a full extent, my humanness and allow you to witness the mysteries behind the veil of the observable and the non-observable world in which we live. Hopefully, you will agree with me that Spirit does work in mysterious ways, bringing us what we need, and revealing to some of us something of a higher spiritual order for the benefit of all. Yes, Spirit's Voice can even be heard through the many and varied miraculous supernatural events that take place in our lives. The following are a few of the ways I heard His Voice.

The Power of Love

Lilacs are for me, the most beautiful, fragrant flower that nature has given us. Every Spring my senses eagerly await the arrival of the sweet, perfumed blossoms. When we moved to our home in the country, I immediately planted a lilac bush in a spot where the winds from the west would blow the sweetness into the open windows of our home. Spring arrived, and the lilac bush had no blossoms on it. Maybe next year it will, I thought. Thirteen Springs passed and still, no lilacs. I contacted the experts in local nurseries and at the Ohio State University Horticulture Department for advice. Apparently, I did everything correctly to ensure blossoms. It should have blossomed a year or two at the most after planting the lilac bush.

The fourteenth Spring, my son and I were talking about the lilac bush and he said, "That's it! I'm sick and tired of waiting every Spring for it to bloom. I'm going to chop it down." "No, no," I shouted, "Don't do that." "Oh yes I am" he replied, marching up the driveway to get an ax from the garage. Once the lilac bush was chopped down, all hope for the beautifully fragrant lilacs is lost, I contemplated. Sadness gripped my heart.

My son arrived with the ax and stood in front of the bush ready to chop it away to oblivion. "Wait," I cried. "Put your ax down a minute. I want to show you something. Watch what the power of love can do." Stepping inside the bush, I put my arms all around the branches as far as I could reach. My son looked at me with a startled expression on his face as I started talking to the lilac bush. "You are so beautiful," I said. "God made you. Deep within you, God has given you the potential to bear the sweetest perfumed purple flowers. You can bring forth your aromatic nectar of His Love within you so that we will all be refreshed and enjoy God's blessings. You have been keeping it locked away inside of you for such a long time. Why don't you just let it come forth? I love you so much and so does God, and that is why God created you."

Stepping away from the bush I said to my son, "This lilac bush is going to bloom this year." "No it isn't," he answered. "Promise me you won't chop it down because I promise you it will bloom this year," I added. With a cocky reply and shaking his head, he picked up the ax and took it back to the garage.

Several weeks later, my son breathlessly bolted into the house calling, "Mom, the lilac bush, come and see the lilac bush!" We both ran as fast as we could, and there it stood, in full glory, lilac blossoms covering the entire twelve-foot bush. The sweet nectar filled our nostrils to capacity as our fingers caressed the exquisite, delicate purple flowers. My eyes released tears of joy and looking tenderly at my son, I said, "See what the power of love can do?" "I have to admit Mom," he said, "Something happened here."

That lilac bush was a powerful witness to my son's spirituality in a way that he could not explain why in any logical sense. He had actually witnessed with his own eyes, the mysterious power of Divine Love. Beyond the boundaries of the universe, we were acquainted with the Divine life-force sweetly standing before us.

Dear friend, be aware that within you resides the substance of unlimited potential awaiting your awareness to bring it into form. There are no impossibilities when you call upon Spirit for help in manifesting them.

Promise Me

In this particular dream, I was in a German concentration camp walking alongside another woman. We were herded into a building and just before the door was locked, she pushed me out and said, "Tell Jake that I'm very happy, and above all, tell him it's all right for him to find happiness again. Do you promise to do that for me?" With my eyes tenderly looking into hers, I said, "I promise." At that same moment someone slammed the door shut and locked it, leaving her inside as I stood outside the building. The dream ended.

Two days later my husband came home from work and announced that Jake's wife died. I didn't know her and only casually knew Jake as a co-worker of Dean's. We went to the funeral service and while the minister was delivering the eulogy for Jake's wife, he mentioned that she was Italian and proceeded to describe the life she had led while in Italy and then later when she married Jake.

Listening politely to the minister's words, I heard him say something that would rattle the bones inside of me. He recalled a time during her life she spent in a German concentration camp. Shocked by what I had just heard, I immediately thought of my dream and my promise to Jake's wife. How would I tell him and when? I wondered. Would he think I was crazy if I talked about my dream with him? It is not easy to step out in faith and assume everyone will believe what I tell him or her, especially when it deals with the unobservable reality. I was very reluctant to tell him the day of her funeral, so I didn't.

Several months later, my husband and I attended his

company's Christmas party. Coincidentally, seated at our table directly across from me were Jake and his female guest. Both of them, in their late sixties, held hands and talked intimately like sweet lovebirds to one another. It was apparent they were very much in love. I knew it was now or never. I had to tell Jake about my dream. Excusing myself from the table, I told Dean I was going to talk with Jake for a little while. Nervously, I knelt down beside Jake and took his hand in mine and said, "Jake, I'm going to tell you something, and you may dismiss what I am going to say as being fanatical, lunacy or whatever, but I have to tell you. I proceeded to tell him that his wife appeared to me in a dream and made me promise to tell him she is very happy and above all, she wants him to find happiness again. When he heard that, Jake spontaneously burst into tears. I looked at Dean sitting across from us, and he had a wrinkled brow that said, "What did you do to Jake to make him cry?" With his eyes, Dean motioned me to come back to my chair, but I knew I had to stay with Jake a few moments longer.

Jake pressed his hands over mine and cried, "Oh God, this is a miracle happening! You did the right thing by telling me. I can't thank you enough." He proceeded to tell me during the summer shortly after his wife died, he went back to his high school reunion in Iowa. At that time, he met the woman who was seated beside him at the Christmas party. Apparently, they had been high school lovers and hadn't seen one another since then. She never married because Jake had been her only true love. She and Jake married shortly afterward.

Looking into my eyes, his eyes soaked with tears, Jake told me, "You had no idea I was dealing with a lot of guilt because I remarried so quickly after my wife's death. I felt guilty about finding happiness with another woman, and it was tearing me up inside." He went on to say that he now believed that his wife was bringing him a message from the beyond to let him know that it's okay to be happy. Jake was elated, and his tear-filled eyes expressed such gratitude to me for sharing this message with him. That evening his guilt was replaced with genuine freedom to love again and to be loved. A healing had indeed taken place that evening, and I felt privileged to have witnessed and honored it. If I had not listened to Spirit's Voice within, I would have passed up the opportunity to express my Divine gift, that of bringing Light, and comfort to others.

Dear friend, Spirit's Voice encourages us to care for others and when we do, greater gifts are given to us to be used for the well-being of humanity. When we fine-tune our heart to listen to His Voice, we will be uplifted to truly recognize Spirit's wondrous Love for us. There is no limit to the power of God's gifts; there is no limit to the service we may give, and we cannot be happy until we give it.

I Saved the Last Dance for You

Earlier in the book I mentioned that I was an Arthur Murray dance instructor for awhile. My dance partner BG, was a wonderful human being whose life greatly impacted mine. When I moved to Ohio, BG and his wife moved to Texas, and we lost touch with one another except for the exchange of Christmas cards every year.

On May 29, 1988, I had a wonderful dream about BG. We were dancing once again all the glorious dances that we had performed together as partners in the early 1960's. The rhythmic Latin dances like the mambo, tango, samba, cha cha, and rhumba, the graceful, fluid motions of the Viennese waltz, the foxtrot, and the rigorous moves of the quickstep and swing; we danced them all in my dream.

What a thrilling experience it was to discover (in my dream) that I possessed all the balance, control, and rhythm that I once had as a spry young woman. We whirled around the dance floor as a single unit of energy, the way Fred Astaire and Ginger Rogers magically danced together. I felt exhilarated beyond words. You see, I stopped dancing completely when I moved to Ohio, and now all that remains is only a dim memory of that happy time in my life.

But here I was in my dream, dancing with my partner as if the interim years never existed. Time stood still for a few brief moments. We were having a marvelous time dancing together when suddenly he said to me, "I have to go now; I won't be back again. I won't see you anymore, but I wanted to save the last dance for you. But the dance of all dances has been my life shared with my wife all these years. I have been very happy with her. I am going to be okay so don't worry about me. I have to go now, I love you." I hugged him with the biggest hug possible, and then he walked away, and I awoke from my dream.

The next day was May 30, Memorial Day. I had not made any plans to celebrate the holiday because my family and I were very busy rebuilding our home after a fire completely destroyed it. We were spending all available time working at the job site, and it was a very tiring job, that's for sure. Yet, I awoke from my dream in such a festive mood, as if I were actually celebrating something. I kept thinking how special that dream was because it was so vivid and so **real**. All day long, my body felt deliriously energized by the dancing we did together in my dream, as if all my cells still retained those past memories. I was so enthralled to have danced again with BG even if it was "only a dream," I reasoned.

All day long, the energy impacted me in such a profound way that even when I was hammering nails or carrying the lumber, I performed those tasks with such love and joy in my heart. Why I even kicked up my heels a few times when no one was looking and whirled around the grass clutching an old broom for a dance partner. On a holiday when I couldn't spare the time to celebrate, in some quiet secret way, I was truly celebrating the love of my special friend BG and the common love of the dance that we shared together so many years earlier. Three months later, I received a note from BG's wife informing me that he had died on May 30 from lung cancer. There is no doubt in my mind that love continues to exist beyond space and time. Love never dies! I am so grateful for these experiences so that I can witness to the fact that life is more than we can witness with our five senses. Life becomes a melody of song and dance when we are able to hear His Voice through the many natural and supernatural ways that Spirit brings forth its love.

Dear friend, Divine Love chose to express itself to you as joy. Let joy become your friend and partner. Dance with joy; sing with joy; live with joy. In the depth of your being you will find joy. Go there and be filled with Divine Joy.

Nancy, Help Me!

For several years my favorite hair stylist was a young woman in her early twenties who worked at a salon that I frequented. In the course of our friendship, we developed a trust and confidence that allowed us to talk freely about matters of our hearts. Since I am very interested and active in near-death studies, it was natural for me to share this information with her. She was very interested in learning about these experiences because she once told me, "It sounds so neat." So we talked a lot about the subject and about my near-death and near-death-like experiences.

One day in the summer of 1988, when I went to the salon to get my hair cut, she announced that this would be her last time to cut my hair as she was planning to move with her boyfriend to the Bahamas and open a salon there. One evening near the date of the day she and her boyfriend were scheduled to fly to the Bahamas, I had a dream about her. I saw her face in front of me, and she was crying hysterically. Sobbing uncontrollably, she screamed, "My boyfriend left me. He isn't with me, and I don't know what I'm going to do. Help me! I'm by myself and I don't know what to do."

I responded very calmly by telling her, "Don't worry, you are going to be all right. Calm down. You're okay; you're okay." She began to stop crying and regained her composure, but she was very concerned about her boyfriend not being with her. Since I didn't see any other images in the dream except my friend's face, I didn't have the benefit of gathering additional information from the surrounding scenes. All I was going on was what she was telling me and the emotional state that she was experiencing. I kept reassuring her that she would be all right, and every time I said that, she seemed to calm down. I told her that she would soon be making a very big decision, but she was not to worry about making the decision. The decision that she would make would be the best decision for her and the right one.

She listened very intently to my words of wisdom and seemed to respect my advice a great deal. I told her not to worry about her boyfriend, and the decision she would make would be independent of her boyfriend. I also told her that she would find great strength within to choose the kind of life she wanted for herself.

At first, she didn't believe that she had any strength because she was feeling very vulnerable and alone, but once again, I reassured her that deep within her was a part of herself that could take good care of her if she would simply trust it. Then, I got the impression that she was beginning to feel more courageous and strengthened to make her important decision. Her face radiated a confidence in place of the fear described earlier. She thanked me for being there when she needed me. I told her I loved her, and she would be fine.

I awoke from the dream in the morning and because so many of my dreams come true, I have learned through the years to listen to the feelings I experience upon waking. If the dream somehow speaks to my inner intuitive self, and I am left with the feeling that the dream is true, then it usually is. My feelings that morning spoke to my inner being in such a way that I knew that she was in trouble, and I had great concern for her. I kept thinking about her and wondered if she made it to the Bahamas with her boyfriend safely or whether he may have abandoned her alone for some reason.

Several weeks later, I made an appointment with a new hair stylist in the same hair salon. One of the first things I said to him was, "Did Sally make it to the Bahamas all right?" There was no response. I continued, "I had a dream about her a few weeks ago and I dreamed that she got into some trouble. My dreams usually come true, and I am very concerned about her." His reply was, "Yes, Sally did get into some trouble. I'll tell you all about it when I'm through cutting your hair," he said.

After my hair was cut, he quietly led me into a private office and said, "I'm curious about your dream; tell me more." So, I told him the whole story. With a rather pained expression on his face, he then informed me that a few days prior to leaving for the Bahamas, she and her boyfriend were killed in an automobile accident. She died first and her boyfriend clung to life for about one half hour and then died.

This is a fascinating account because evidently, I was communicating with her as she was leaving her body to make her transition to the next life. Her concern for her boyfriend was obvious. I felt privileged to have had the opportunity to help her make the transition to the other side if that was the choice she wanted to make. Apparently, she reached out to me because of our discussions about near-death experiences, and she knew I would help her in this situation. We are never alone at the moment of our death. Love will always take our hand and walk with us.

Dear friend, nothing can separate you from the gift of Spirit's Presence within you. Nearer to you than your heartbeat, the center of your being is where God lives. God will never, ever, leave you or forsake you no matter what you have done or failed to do. Be aware of this Holy Presence. Claim the Holy Presence within you. You will never be alone!

Goodbye, Dear Friend

This account is of a young man who committed suicide in 1989. He was the son of John, our dear friend who died in January 1979 when his plane crashed flying over the Alaskan tundra. Austin had a great deal of difficulty accepting the death of his father, and he was a very tormented soul for many years. Unaware of Austin's death on the night of his suicide, I had a dream about him. In the dream, I was walking into his bedroom where he was sitting. The moment he saw me his eyes lit up, and he bolted from his chair embracing me with a big bear hug. "Nancy," he said, "Thank you so much for being such a good friend to me for all these years. I love you very much. You always loved me so unconditionally, and I want you to know how much I treasured that kind of love."

I was so touched by his sweet words and tenderly looking into his eyes, I said to him, "You were like a son to me so it was easy to love you so much." Austin replied, "No, your love was pure love, something I never received from anyone else. Your love was so special and so are you."

We hugged again and then he said, "I have to go now and go back to where I live." Instantly, I was confused because the scene was taking place in the bedroom of his home, and I thought he was mistaken somehow. He immediately read my thoughts and said, "No, this is not where I live any longer." He pointed upward and when I looked up, the roof of his house was missing. I could see the vast universe with the stars and planets shining so brightly above. "That's where I live now," he said.

With a deep, intuitive understanding, I knew that he was telling me the truth and that soon he had to leave. I told him that I understood, and that it was okay if he had to leave. At least we were sharing a loving moment together and telling one another how deeply our lives had touched one another. We both felt tremendous joy in communicating our love for each other. Suddenly, after our last hug, he flew upward into the dark universe, and I watched him fade away. I felt at peace. The dream ended. The next morning, the feelings that the dream imparted were strong. My immediate reaction was to call him on the telephone and see how he was, but a few hours later, his family called and told me that he had committed suicide **in his bedroom** the night before.

I will always be grateful for the visions in my dreams from those wanting to bring a message to me or to others because it confirms the veil connecting the physical realm with the spiritual realm is a thin one. It confirms the fact that love knows no barriers and that love is stronger than death itself.

Dear friend, the love that passes between the children of God is a cherished gift of Divine Grace that we may be one. The Spirit of Love is eternal and never dies. The spirits of our loved ones know the reality of the continuity of life and have a clear vision that love is eternal. Time and space are no deterrents to eternal love and communication with our loved ones for there is no separation in Spirit. All live in Divine Spirit whether it is in this world or beyond.

How Can This Be Explained?

If anyone can explain how this can happen, I'd like to know because I can't explain it. One evening I had a dream. I was seated in a large auditorium awaiting to hear a concert in which a song that I wrote would be performed by an orchestra. The crowd of people were filing down the aisles anticipating a wonderful concert that evening, and I was very excited that the song I had composed would be one of the attractions this crowd had come to hear.

The lights in the auditorium dimmed; the audience quieted, and the curtains opened to reveal the musicians and their instruments on stage. The first notes on their instruments sounded, and I recognized they were beginning to play the song I had composed. My heart swelled with gratification for composing such a beautiful song, and I was overjoyed when the audience applauded loudly to voice their pleasure.

I awoke from the dream in the morning and throughout the entire day I caught myself humming that song. I just couldn't get it off my mind. I kept thinking that this song could be a hit song; it was that good. Over and over I would hum the song during the next days and weeks. I couldn't get it off my mind.

My friend called me one day, and I told her about this song that I couldn't get out of my mind, and that I was humming it all day long. Since I don't read music, I couldn't write the notes down on paper so I got my tape recorder and hummed the song into it so I would never forget it. I thought that one day I could let someone listen to the recording, and if they knew how to transpose the music into notes, then perhaps I would be able to do something with the song. I believed so strongly that this song would become a hit song one day.

One year later for my birthday, my husband took me to a music concert by Kitaro, a Japanese new-age musician. I was so excited to be attending a live concert featuring his wonderful music. My husband and I were filing down the aisle to take our seats along with hundreds of other audience members that came to the Ohio Theater that evening. You could feel the anticipation of everyone ready to enjoy a live concert by Kitaro and his musicians.

A man's voice suddenly came through a loudspeaker to bring the audience an important message. "Good evening ladies and gentlemen, welcome to the Ohio Theater for a very special concert by Kitaro. This is Kitaro's very first concert in the

United States, and we are very pleased that he chose to come to Columbus, Ohio for his first concert. I want to let you know that the music Kitaro will be playing for you this evening is from his new album. Kojiki. However, there aren't any albums available for sale yet in the United States so please wait a few weeks until shipments are made to your stores before you try purchasing them. Now, let's go on with the show."

The audience was hushed. I was sitting on the edge of my seat eagerly waiting for the curtain to open, and I would see Kitaro and his musicians live on stage. Wow, was I excited! Then it happened; the curtain opened and the audience burst out in applause to welcome Kitaro. He acknowledged the audience with a nod and instructed his musicians to begin playing. I cannot find the words to describe what I heard next. As each individual note played, I recognized that it was MY SONG, the song I had composed in my dream one year earlier! How can this be? This is impossible! The entire dream I had one year earlier was taking place before me right then and there. If that wasn't enough of a shock to me, while the music was playing the song so beautifully, a golden light fed by a laser beam was hovering over the audience like a giant cloud of love. Disbelief, gratitude, love, joy, all the feelings intermingled with one another, and I couldn't contain my feelings of overwhelming joy anymore so I cried softly trying not to call attention to myself. I felt the presence of the Divine as if the Light was watching over us as the music played on and on.

Afterwards, I told my husband about the dream I had one year earlier and what happened at the concert we attended. My husband told me that I probably heard that song on the radio prior to my dream, and there was nothing supernatural going on. "No, no," I said. "Remember what the man on the loud-speaker at the concert said before the show began? He said this is Kitaro's very first appearance in the United States, and there were no albums (Kojiki) in the country yet. Besides, I had the dream one year earlier before he made his album with the song on it."

My husband just laughed and said there is an obvious explanation for this but when I asked him to give me one, he couldn't.

I want to be very clear about this. I do not want any claim to nor do I profess to have composed that song before Kitaro did. This is Kitaro's song, plain and simple. The only thing I am interested in is how my mind/dream was somehow connected to Kitaro and his song in that mysterious way one year before I actually heard the song in the physical reality. If anyone can enlighten me, please email me with your idea. **nancyclarkauthor@gmail.com** Thank you.

Dear friend, love can be found everywhere, yes, even in a song. The energy of love knows no boundaries so look for it everywhere in your little corner of the world. It will find you and bless you with such sweet surprises.

CHAPTER 12

CONVERSATIONS WITH GOD

So many of our thoughts are blind to the Heavenly secrets of God. We shall be made truly wise if we enter into the silence to find that Sacred place and letting the incomparable gift of God's Voice speak within.

Throughout the years following my return from Heaven's Door, I have been guided spiritually, nurtured, and encouraged on my journey with the Divine in a way that defies explanation. Because we were created so uniquely and individually, our Creator knows us better than we know ourselves. I have an analytical mind that often times questions whether I am indeed receiving Divine Inspiration, or if I am simply being guided by my own ego-driven self. If I am skeptical, my impulse is to dismiss the information.

A method had to be in place that would remove all doubt about whose guidance I was following, my own or the Divine. If I truly seek to follow Divine Guidance, and Spirit knows this, then by Divine Grace, a way will be provided. The method that I was shown completely eradicates any attempt on my part to manipulate the outcome according to my own will. What occurs during this method is the unveiling of Divine Love and Divine Guidance.

Let me explain how I was led to receive this Divine gift. One day I needed guidance for a decision I had to make and I wanted that guidance to come from Divine Source. I prayed earnestly, opening my heart and soul so wide to God. I asked for a sign so that I would be absolutely certain the answer would be the **Divine Guidance** I was seeking. With closed eyes, I anxiously awaited a sign. I didn't know what to expect. Perhaps I would have another experience like I had at John's funeral service. That experience was absolute truth for me. I needed **absolute truth** to resolve my dilemma. I waited. Nothing happened. Opening my eyes, I glanced toward the bookshelf and saw a Bible I had recently purchased with the intent of reading it one day. I grasped the book and thought, the answer must be somewhere in that Bible, but I never read the Bible and wouldn't know how to find the answer to my question in it.

Guided by intuition, I held the closed Bible over my heart and with a genuine, heartfelt petition, I asked God to lead me to a passage that would speak to my heart and would answer my question. I closed my eyes and still holding the closed Bible over my heart, I took my right index finger and held it several inches above the closed pages. My finger began to move in a back and forth motion. In my thoughts, I wondered how would I know when to open the book. Then suddenly, in the corner of my left eye, I saw a flash of white light. That's different, I thought. Immediately, and still with closed eyes, I poked my index finger into the closed pages.

What followed was such a sacred moment in my life as I read the Holy words on the pages. Without any personal intent on my part to manipulate the outcome, there clearly and unmistakably was the answer to the problem I was asking God to help me with. The Bible passage that I was led to spoke *directly to what my problem was about*. Even the words in the specific passage were the same specific words I used during my prayer. With tears pouring from my eyes, the Bible message permeating the depth of my soul, a sense of wonder, awe, and reverence merged into one glorious expression of gratitude for the gift I was receiving. God had heard my need. God had answered that need. God had spoken to me! I heard His Voice! Sobbing by this time from sheer joy, I tried to thank God for the precious gift that I had just received. Words were limited. How do you find words to describe what just happened? I finally gave up speaking the words of appreciation, instead, yielding to the deep inner stirrings of my heart, I lifted up to God every fiber of love I felt for Him. I let my love speak the words I could not say.

After emptying myself completely and letting go of every loving feeling I had, I felt emotionally drained. To me, a miracle had just occurred. I could have turned anywhere in the Bible and the message would have been completely different. It wouldn't have been as **specific** to my particular question and my need to discern the guidance that was deemed for my highest good. The Biblical passage I read that day while snuggled close to the Divine Spirit within, freed my ego's need to control my life. From that day forward, I vowed I would never again put my own misguided ego's needs above Divine Intent. Any paths I take upon my life's journey will always involve spiritual guidance directly from the all-knowing Source, the Higher Power within. I use the Bible in the manner as I did that special day to help me to hear His Voice instead of my own. In my opinion, this form of communication represents a goal-oriented, perfectly orchestrated and extraordinary significant outcome that cannot be construed as coincidence or a random event. Common sense tells us that the odds against something like this happening repeatedly is colossal! Ask a statistician what the odds would be that this method of communication with the Divine happens by chance and nothing more. I am sure the odds would be the same as winning the lottery. One time, two times, I would agree that it was probably the result of chance. But **every time** I close my eyes and open the closed pages of the Bible after seeing a white light in the corner of my eye, I am led to a passage or passages that speak specifically to what I was just praying. In other words, during intense prayer and submission, Spirit speaks to me through the passages that God leads me. **Always**, there is deep reverence toward the One who will guide me toward my highest good. I never use this technique like a psychic tool of sorts, or a technique that does not involve humility, love, and deep, deep communion with the Divine Presence within.

I have used this technique for many years now. The Light is still within me, as it is **in all souls**. The Light is shining its brilliance and casting a beautiful life within me. A channel has been created by Spirit that brings love, healing, and power onto the earth through me. But I am an ordinary woman, not a saint. Becoming a channel for Spirit and awakening to the inner knowledge long buried within **all of us** is what the Light taught me during my near-death-like experience to share with others. There is no separation in Spirit. Spirit gives us love and Spirit receives ours. Spirit will find ways that are specific to our needs to unfold within us continually with beginnings, fulfillments, and levels of consciousness that will allow us to feel the realization of the spiritual nature which is truly ours.

We are all children of the Light from whom all blessings flow. We are neither "deserving or non-deserving." That is conditional love. Think of the process of opening a door. Now, that act is neither good or bad. It is simply a function, which allows you passage into a room. Likewise, the Light has prepared many rooms for us and invites us to enter into the realm of Divine Dwelling. To enter however, the soul must prepare itself spiritually first, recognize there is a door to be opened, and second, to walk in and receive the intended good. LOVE is the key that opens the door. Greed, lust, selfish motives of any kind will never open the door, so one must be very sure his or her motives are based upon a commitment to live one's life in harmony with the Divine Presence within. This kind of harmony results in Divine Union, a fusion that brings forth from itself, Divine Good.

Motives that are unloving create spiritual blinders in the consciousness of someone seeking ultimate good. Those blinders will obscure the Divinity that is present within us. Acting from a base of unloving motives results in a remote distancing from and a replacement of man's will over Divine Will. For many, this is very difficult to do for ego's selfish needs cry out for attention all the time. Divine Love flowing naturally through an individual speaks a soft voice that does not judge, condemn, ridicule, or dominate over anyone in any way.

If you are confused whether you are living your life controlled by your ego needs or are truly living a spiritual life, just ask yourself this question when you begin to act on something. Does this choice or action I am about to take reflect a loving response to Spirit, self, or another? Is this the way Spirit would choose to react? No, you will not be successful all the time in the choices you make. I am not; no one is. But it is not so much the end result that determines your spirituality, more important is the journey to that end. The sincere, honest desire deep within your heart to make the loving response is what matters most of all. As long as we are human beings, we will continually make choices that stem both from ego and spiritual needs. In doing so, however, remember that your choices have a direct correlation to the kind of life that is drawn to you. In my opinion, nothing can outshine the brilliance of a spiritual life lived in and for the Divine Light within.

We are empowered with a deeper intimacy with Spirit as an active partner in our lives, guiding and nurturing us by Divine Grace. With child-like faith, we can approach the One whose love for us surpasses any ideas of imagination. We can establish contact with the Divine with complete trust and confidence that we will be greeted with open arms. We will always know that the Light will provide for us so that in turn, we may share with others what we have been given. It then becomes a continuing circle of Infinite Love emanating from Grace that we pass on to one another. **The Light can be seen when we help one another and touch one another's lives in loving ways.**

You will soon see from the simple communication technique using the Bible passages as guidance from my Great Teacher that the technique has proven itself authentic. I know this gift has nothing to do with my Great Teacher favoring me because I am a "good" person. There are daily reminders of my human weakness. I am not a saint and my Great Teacher knows that. Yet, there is a plan for my life, and I can sense when I am being used to touch others lives in some way. I can see my Great Teacher at work through this book and through all the times when I am called upon to witness to the many ways Spirit communicates with us by revealing many mysterious insights to us. I can see the Light working through others in ways that are vastly different from mine. For every single one of us, this is the intimate miracle of the Light's LOVE working in our lives.

At this time, I would like to share some common examples of the conversations I have had with my Great Teacher when I have used the Bible technique. The method once again is simple. First, I raise my awareness of the Divine Presence within me with sincere, heartfelt prayer. Intimately communing with the Holy One, I share my need to know what guidance I need to receive pertaining to a particular aspect of my life. I might simply ask for comfort, strength, love, or guidance on a decision I must make. There is nothing too insignificant to come before my Great Teacher and ask for help. With closed eyes, I hold the Bible over my heart and ask that I be led to a passage that will speak to my heart about my particular need. Then holding my index finger about two to three inches above the closed book, I begin moving my finger back and forth until I see a white light in the corner of my left eye. Immediately, I poke my finger into the closed pages and ask that I will be given the ability to understand what I will be reading. **Always**, the passage I am led to speaks directly to what I just prayed about - **always**! I am going to open my heart with you now and share some of my intimate conversations with my Great Teacher and show you some of the Bible passages to which I was led with my eyes closed so you can see for yourself how this is not a coincidence but specific to my need at the time. These are Holy moments!

EXAMPLES OF MY CONVERSATIONS WITH GOD

Prayer: "Lord, let me be a pencil in your hand. I ask that you will bring forth your creative power and write this book through me. My only desire is to serve you."

Reply: Matthew 15:28

"You are a woman of great faith! What you want will be done for you."

Prayer: "Lord, I have been invited to lead a spiritual retreat in Virginia and I'm not sure what I should talk about."

Reply: Mark 13:11

"Do not worry ahead of time about what you are going to say; when the time comes, say whatever is then given to you. For the words you speak will not be yours, they will come from the Holy Spirit."

Prayer: Lord, this is the anniversary day of my encounter with you. I promise to do the work you called me to do because I love you above all. Do you have a special message for me on this special day?"

Reply: Acts 26:16-18

"I have appeared to you to appoint you as my servant. You are to tell others what you have seen of me today and what I will show you in the future. You are to open their eyes and turn them from the

darkness to the light and from the power of Satan to God, so that through their faith in me, they will have their sins forgiven and receive their place among God's chosen people."

Prayer: "Lord, a woman phoned me in great spiritual distress. She feels separated from you and feels Satan may have a stronger hold on her. I will tell her what passage you led me to for her guidance."

Reply: Romans 8:38-39

"For I am certain that nothing can separate us from his love; neither death nor life, neither angels nor other heavenly rulers or powers, neither the present nor the future, neither the world above nor the world below - there is nothing in all creation that will ever be able to separate us from the love of God which is ours through Christ Jesus our Lord."

Prayer: "Lord, what shall I tell others seeking your Divine Wisdom?"

Reply: James 1:5-8

"But if any of you lack wisdom, you should pray to God, who will give it to you; because God gives generously and graciously to all. But when you pray, you must believe and not doubt at all. Whoever doubts is like a wave in the sea that is driven and blown about by the wind. If you are like that, unable to make up your mind and undecided in all you do, you must not think that you will receive anything from the Lord."

Prayer: "Lord, please give me a sign in the Bible passage that will tell me if what has come through during these inspired writing sessions with you for this book is an accurate account of your Divine Will."

Reply: John 19:22

"What I have written stays written."

Prayer: "Lord, sometimes I worry that others will not believe that I was with you and that you called me to share your message of love and hope to humanity. Please help to strengthen me on my journey from your Holy Wisdom."

Reply: Luke 10:16 and Luke 10:23-24

"Whoever listens to you listens to me; whoever rejects you rejects me; and whoever rejects me rejects the one who sent me. How fortunate you are to see the things you see! I tell you that many prophets and kings wanted to see what you see, but they could not, and to hear what you hear, but they did not."

Dear friend, I speak words of truth when I tell you that God's Voice can be heard when you allow it to happen within you. Seek to hear His Voice from the depths of your being and know with absolute conviction that Spirit will communicate with you. Because we are loved so much, we are being asked to free ourselves of all resistance and doubt. Enter into the Sacred Power of Love and let that power lift your heart ever closer and closer to Spirit within. **The more love that fills you, the more you will enter into the deeper levels of your being and into direct contact with the Light of God.** What a joy!

CHAPTER 13

REVELATORY WISDOM

*Open your heart, your mind, your soul as much as you can
and let love change the way you perceive your experience of
God and all of life. See through the eyes of your soul.*

After I chose to return back to physical sense reality during
my near-death-like experience, the Light of God telepathically
poured a tremendous amount of knowledge into my consciousness. I cannot recall the cure for diseases or future inventions,
etc., but I do recall what I consider to be spiritual wisdom.
This recall flows through my consciousness only during those
moments when I am actually doing the work I was called to do.
For instance, when I am speaking to audiences, working individually with someone, or writing, the spiritually inspired words
simply flow from me as if I am momentarily being transported
back to my experience and opening a pathway from which the
knowledge flows. This wisdom is not accessible to my analytical, left brain thought processes, and for that reason, I am
often times unable to recall the information upon command.
Perhaps a better way of explaining it would be to simply say,
when I get out of my own way and "let God," do it, the material
flows. When the ego "I," takes charge, nothing happens. I have
not taken courses in religion, spirituality, psychology, new age
philosophies, physics, etc. What I am sharing with you comes

directly from what my Great Teacher revealed to me during my near-death-like experience and from no other outside source.

This book for instance, focuses on the nature of the spiritual design, which is the most important aspect of all that I learned from my Great Teacher. It is the prerequisite preparation of our human hearts to the coming of a new future for the world where one day we will become transformed and empowered with the love of the Divine Eternal Presence among us. Listen carefully and hear His Voice in the inspired words that follow.

BEGINNINGS

Many fear that the end will soon come. But the "end" must be redefined. If, as many think the end means termination, this is in err. There can be no ending when there are only beginnings. What we think of as endings, are really beginnings, simply a change in direction and motion. New life evolves that is only different in form from what once was recognized and perceived through the physical senses. This is why man's ability to understand the workings of the cosmos is so limited. Always, we are headed on an evolutionary thrust forward. Our destination is the return "home" to our true understanding of who we are within. Until we attain that state of enlightenment, we shall always be searching and seeking. Our hearts will remain polarized as we are drawn first this way and then that way, yearning to seek attachment so that we are not floundering aimlessly with no destination in sight.

Beginnings are meant to bridge the boundaries of the unseen with the seen. To the closed mind there will be no sight, no destination to view. But with hearts lifted in hope, raised in faith to the level of expectation, lives are then charted upon a destination that sees no end, sees no adversities, sees no lies, and sees only truth. When one begins to see through the eyes of love, it is impossible to see anything except its own familiar recognition of itself. Truth has stood the hands of time since the beginning of creation and truth will continue to prevail through the seasons of many creations to come.

In our limited awareness, we do not want to accept ultimate reality because in doing so, it causes us to release ourselves fully into the network of the universe from which we have emerged. While this is the desired state of being, we are fearful that we will be lost in the homogeneous mixture of creation. Ego needs within the human being are very powerful energy needs that seek separation rather than unification. If mankind will only trust that there is a better way, a more knowing way, a more loving way than our own limited ego needs, he/she would be propelled upward on a new beginning of the journey toward the Creator one calls God.

For those who have come directly into contact with the Divine, those lives have been changed forever. Never again will they be drawn toward limited thinking, selfish needs, hatred, intolerance, or any other unloving ways of action. Rather, they will be uplifted to a new level of peace, contemplation, where there is a condition known to exist that supersedes any imagined ideas of paradise. To return "home" is to have similar mind consciousness as the Divine, but first we must begin the process of transforming our limited awareness. The very fabric and structure of creation is Spirit, and it is our Spirit and not our bodies that are created in the image and likeness of God.

In order to reach the source of our Higher Powers where we can avail ourselves of the wisdom needed to shed light on all our problems, we must develop our soul. We need our soul to supply vital nourishment to our mind to keep us healthy. Soul reveals inspiration, truth, and understanding. If we only avail ourselves to our ego's needs of desire, self-love, pride and so on, we would be led into purposeless ways, which chokes out our authentic individuality. This lower side of our nature assimilates our life experiences by means of reason, judgment, and analysis through our intellect. We need ego as the foundation for the cultivation of our higher gifts and discrimination to provide a base for our added knowledge. But knowledge, unless it is augmented by wisdom, will stifle the revelations needed for spiritual growth.

We were created with the potential of exhilarating qualities as a human being, a soul functioning openly and unobstructed through a wholesome body resulting in a life that brings us true joy and happiness. Too many of us ignore soul-consciousness through lack of understanding, or we consider it insignificant to the preference of our intellect. My former life was scientifically oriented. I knew nothing of soul-consciousness whereby soul is actively working through the physical body to reveal its Divine attributes and express its wonders to those on earth. My religious orientation taught me that the soul is something inside of us that survives the death of the physical body and transcends to either Heaven or Hell, depending on how good a life we had lived. That's basically all I knew about the soul. It wasn't until my near-death-like experience in 1979 that the Light revealed all the knowledge of the soul to me and gave me instructions to share that knowledge with others. I promised I would do this, and this is why I am writing this book.

My Great Teacher taught me that the true heart of man is not in the flesh but is in the soul. In order to carry on life in the material world, it is necessary for the soul to express through physical matter those realities we call love, wisdom, and power. When we develop the inner awareness of soul, it fosters perfect harmony and spiritual kinship, inspiring us spiritually, mentally, and physically.

My near-death-like experience through its intrinsic forces awakened within me the conviction and the lucidity of that inner sanctuary where the Voice of Divine Spirit resides. It was a priceless revelation of a power indescribable that erased my physical semblance of reality and replaced it with the true essence of reality. I say semblance of reality because our minds perceive us to be very limited human beings, composed and restricted by matter, suffering, delusion, inertia, fears, and doubts.

The only way to show you that the illusions of the conditions of our world can be changed is to prove them by realizing them. This means that we can develop the powers of our soul and endow ourselves with the personality through which life forces can flow with ease. If we have the courage to begin to listen to the inspirational Voice within, then nothing in this world is impossible, for Spirit has performed miracles before and will continue for infinity because of Spirit's unconditional love for us.

Too many of us live our lives shackled to the past by our misperceptions of reality based on fear and guilt. Who hasn't experienced this? We all have of course. At the deep unconscious level, we perceive ourselves to be separate from God and one another. We doubt that we are worthy human beings and as a result, we are always trying to prove our worthiness by the goals we set for ourselves and by cherishing the accumulation of treasures in our external world. We also accept the concept of guilt, and we punish ourselves by making choices that guarantee our unhappiness.

One of the greatest light bulb moments of my experience was when my Great Teacher taught me that I am not separate from God. The separation and guilt is only a misperception in the minds of men, an error to be corrected not punished. This misperception hides the reality of our true being. This is so important to understand because during my experience, my Great Teacher told me that mankind is blaming God for everything that is bad, as if it is "God's Will" that bad things happen to good people. We use God as our scapegoat and dump all the responsibility on Him. What a raw deal, I thought as my new understanding of God was taking hold.

This was a new beginning for me in my perception of God and reality. My Great Teacher infused me with the truth of the Light's unconditional love, and this knowledge is what Spirit wanted me to promulgate to my brothers and sisters once I returned to the physical realm. Listen to His Voice carefully so that you can begin to change your misperception about God as well.

We were created in the image of God, and God is perfect. God is Love; God is Holy. God's Holiness is within us, hidden from us only by our own misperception that we are separated from God. We were created to be extensions of the Light of God by extending the Light's love and by co-creating with the Light to heal the misperceptions and separation that exists in our minds. We were given the Holy Spirit which resides within us to help us remove the barriers from our realization of who we really are, God's Holy and perfect children. Spirit allows us to experience Divine perfect love that we have hidden from ourselves. Spirit takes us by the hand and leads us home.

What is the Light trying to tell us? Be all that we were created to be! Erase the mistaken beliefs that chain us to the past claiming that we are less than we were created to be. Divine Perfect Love cannot radiate in the presence of fear or guilt, so let us begin with a conscious willingness to let go and let Spirit help us. Spirit will respond to us when we have fervently set our mind upon the One who loves us so unconditionally. In the inner sanctum of our heart there must be the absolute conviction that Spirit will respond to us. If we don't feel Peace, Love, or Joy, it is because we are being tested to see if we are being truthful in affirming our desire for the Divine Presence. Partial longing doesn't count. We must convince the Holy One of our need for Him with every fiber of our being. Such devotion to our beloved Creator will attract His attention, and you will find Him.

Dear friend, begin today, this moment, to remove the veil that clouds the elusive vision of your true identity just as I did during my own experience. Awaken to the cherished gift of Divine Oneness within you. Receive the Holy Love. Receive the Holy Light and perceive what God has intended for you to perceive.

THE ENERGY OF THE LIGHT

Science has clearly determined that everything in the physical realm may be reduced to energy. Everything that is composed of matter is energy. Matter is reducible to atoms and atoms are known to be energy. Energy is always in motion, vibrating at a frequency which can be measured by so many cycles per second. It is my understanding for example, that long wave radio is in the energy band of a few thousand cycles per second. That rate of vibration is so high that our minds have difficulty comprehending that figure.

A much higher energy vibration exists that is part of the band beyond what has so far been detected, and our souls are composed of it. This spiritual energy comes directly from the great Designer of Life in the plan our Creator had for the evolution of mankind in order that we can develop the attributes of a living soul, the growth which entitles all of us to become a vehicle for Divine Expression. This treasure lies buried in consciousness waiting for us to open the door and find its power to furnish enlightenment. When we begin to use this form of energy, we will become enlightened beings, able to know without a shadow of a doubt that we can utilize principles and create by them a living reality.

The most powerful energy force that man has available to him to harness and utilize is consciousness. We are directly connected to the Light within us by the power of our thoughts. When a thought occurs, energy becomes available to us to create subsequent forms. Created form originates first in thought form from the energy originating from the Light of God. What first originates in thought form is then created, not the other way around. Mankind will progress faster in our evolutionary development when we can realize that the energy of thought is more powerful than the created forms such as turbines, diesels, nuclear energy, or any other defined physical energy known to man.

The power that is generated behind belief and faith is the same spiritual power the cosmos created unto itself from the Creator. This is the *purest* energy of Divine Light, and it must always give of itself, from its own Source. Because we are part of that purest energy of Divine Light, our faith and our prayers are also the most powerful energies in the universe.

There is an underlying motive for love, unity, and harmony flowing continually from the Light of God outwardly like open arms reaching out to embrace what lies before it. If mankind truly desires to exist in harmony with the universe, mankind must begin to recognize that it cannot live outside of its own Source of pure Divine Light. When we begin to fully comprehend the thought that we are co-creators of the universe with our Creator through the energy of our thoughts, mankind will be able to take more responsibility in creating the kind of world that is in keeping with universal laws.

In order to understand how Spirit works, we must first comprehend love in its deepest meaning. The energy of the Light is called **LOVE**. All things are made known to all of us, but to tap into this great understanding of the perfection of the universe, one must consciously align oneself to the energy of **LOVE**. There is no other way. All things will be mysterious and will appear to be hidden when one is out of synchronization with Divine Love. Change the thought from an unloving one to a loving one, and you immediately align yourself to the free flowing energy of the Divine Life within you. At that point, the Biblical passage, *"With God, all things are possible,"* (Matthew 7:7) becomes actualized.

Your real self is your soul, the Light's unconditional love implanted in the human being in order for us to experience the flowing of the essence of the Divine Reality in our lives. Love can only emanate from its Source, God, for God is Love. Radiating from Spirit, love can produce only good, never evil. That is why it is so important to recognize the source of your love within. When we feel genuine, heartfelt love and gratitude toward our creator, our soul opens up to receive even greater gifts for we are in direct contact with our Divine Inheritance at that point.

Because we are all a connecting link to the spiritual energy that produces only beauty and goodness, we must learn to live more in the spiritual body; most of us only fathom the physical body as the accepted reality. We can increase or decrease the energy of our Light within by our intentions and the choices we make. Producing the right inner conditions allows the energy of the soul to reveal in our lives that transforming essence of being, which gives us the power to evolve into our Higher Divine Selves.

Spirit flowing freely, permeates all which it contacts. It is this radiant Light of the soul, a breath of God manifesting in a human being which makes life vital and worth the living. Happiness is the by-product of our soul expressing those living realities, which we call love, wisdom, and power. I have never wanted anything so much as to see others working toward the ultimate realization of our infinite possibilities. When we begin to wonder what lies beyond the mountain and our desires beckon us to climb upward, we begin to see new proof of our larger vision.

How often do we pass the time daydreaming and wishing we could render a better life for ourselves. We sit and wait for some magic wand to appear to transform the ugliness into beauty, chaos into order, weakness into strength. But nothing happens. One of the most astonishing bits of knowledge that I was given during my near-death-like experience is that the energy of imagination is reality in the making. Our hopes and dreams can gradually be evolved into a material substance when we remember that God

OUR NEED TO BE LOVED

Human beings are a frail species, sensitive to peers and the pressure they assert. We have a natural tendency to want to conform to the whole in order to feel accepted. We identify ourselves based upon the observations of others. So great is our need to conform that many persons assume the identities, habits, and traits of the majority. So long as the majorities have found an accepted role in society, other individuals will seek to follow after and mold themselves into the perceived ideal. Often times, they will go to extremes in order to feel a part of the whole. Some may join gangs and commit crimes in order to be accepted by their peers. To some, it doesn't matter if it is right or wrong as long as they are included in the group.

This need to feel union with other human beings is a primitive need originating from the time of birth. A baby's primary need is to be loved. Mirasmus is a term the American Medical Association uses to describe those infants who die from not receiving any physical contact or love even though their nutritional needs have been met. Love is the sustaining breath of life itself! Our need to be loved is the basis of the foundation of our being, and we will go to great lengths in pursuit of this need. A young baby knows instinctively that it needs to be loved, and it is uninhibited in its quest. It will cry when it needs to be held and loved. At times, we must become like a baby and cry out incessantly to our Parent of all Parents until our cries have been heard. God will hold us and comfort us just as a mother would comfort her baby.

There is a louder voice, however, that clamors above all other voices within. I am speaking of the ego. Human beings have a need to feel an identification with self that is all-inclusive. Forming an image of itself, the ego is able to define, regulate, and control the energy of thought and action within the confines of self. The result is that the self has created a limited view of itself and is fearful to attach to itself to anything else that exceeds the perceived definition of itself. Hence, the self fails to grow toward the realization that it is more than it can see, taste, smell, touch, or hear. The self has chosen to be locked into a consciousness awareness that is lacking in a higher state of perception.

The self begins to masquerade behind a costume of fear, guilt, unworthiness, and a belief that it is not capable of loving or being loved. The result of this illusion is a life filled with turmoil and a feeling of separation from the Divine, self, and others. When one is able to cast aside this false self and acknowledge the true self, one is freed from the chains of torment and separation and is then able to genuinely love and be loved without measure, boundaries or limits.

To find love in its deepest intimacy, we begin by discovering the loving powers of our own soul. Divine Love within us as Spirit is limitless, and if we truly desire to find it, we must trust our soul to bring it to us. Then one of the greatest gifts which man is endowed shall become a real blessing to him, shaping his desires according to his soul's needs, and revealing the radiance of Divine Intent. Developing the power to perceive the Divine Love within means that you are true to your higher self and can be entrusted with the wisdom to bring about different conditions in your world if you wish to do so.

People who are unaware of their own Divine Love residing within and the power that love can generate to transform their lives are left to work out every problem by means of ego and mind. These lesser resources are constricted by matter and inhibited by anguish, confusion, and emotion. The fact is that the stumbling blocks we encounter are self-made and usually the result of a biased mind in some fashion. The free flow of the soul's intrinsic loving wisdom cannot reach the mind unless that mind has sufficiently opened itself up to receive soul's higher knowledge.

Our need to be loved is God within us making His Voice known to us. Our soul is the very breath of Divine Life that seeks to liberate and enter us into a new realm of reality, where we reach out for love and truth, which in turn, enables us to surmount obstacles that once had been barriers to our happiness. Listen to His Voice within to find the love of infinite tenderness that assures us of God's constant concern for us.

Spirit's Voice within us is that part of our soul which motivates us toward kindly impulses that beckon us to reach out our hands to comfort and help those in need. Seeking no reward and acting only from a desire of service, we reveal our Essence of Being to ourselves and to others. Wherever we go, we will carry within our hearts the joyful awareness of the Holy Presence.

Dear friend, open your whole heart to the indwelling all-encompassing love that the Light has intended for you to perceive. When you want it bad enough, you will find it. Absorb all of it, wrapping yourself in peace and fulfillment knowing that it is your gift from the Light to feel, express, and to be the Love of God. Never let anyone or anything make you feel separated from this Love! No matter what trials course through your life, Divine Love is living with you to enrich your life and the lives of others. Dwell always within this Divine Love finding love everywhere, in everything, in everyone. Help others to see their love within them for Spirit gives the same love to all. We are all called to spread the love of Spirit for it is through oneness that we grow in our awareness of God's Love in the world.

WE ARE ALL RAYS OF LIGHT

Love will never be contained because of the nature of love. Its expression is one of freedom and movement. It seeks to flow away from itself as a ray of Light to someone or something else. When it is received and accepted, the total sum energy of love becomes stronger. To give and to receive fulfills the cycle.

No one will argue the fact that kindness, compassion, and love are indeed, vital and necessary to our well-being. But we tend to think of love as an emotion rather than the true energy that it is - the actual energy of the Light of God. We do not yet understand that when we are tapping into the power source of Divine Love, we enable the life force within us to expand to a capacity beyond comprehension of our limited awareness.

The expansion of this Divine Love touched me in a very deep and meaningful way one rainy Spring morning following our house fire. We were renting a home in the country while rebuilding our home, and I was getting ready to leave for the job site when I heard a loud knock on the kitchen door. There stood an elderly woman, perhaps in her eighties, wearing a tattered blue raincoat and holding a small plastic trash bag on top of her head to keep her glistening gray hair dry.

I opened the door and she asked, "Are you Mrs. Clark, the woman whose house burned down?" With a curious look on my face, I replied, "Yes." "Well Mrs. Clark, I heard about your tragedy in my church. Although I don't have much, I wanted to bring you something." Then slowly reaching her stiff, arthritic hand into her coat pocket, she pulled out a small metal object and placed it so lovingly into my hand. With a tender smile on her face, she said, "If you are a woman who likes to sew, then I know you can't sew unless you use a thimble. I want you to have mine."

My eyes gazed down at the small silver thimble that she had placed so delicately in my hand, and I noticed that it was very old. The metal had been worn down in several places, obviously from many years of personal use. Then quickly, she told me she had to go because her friend who drove her to my house was waiting in the car and had another appointment. I hugged her and told her how much I appreciated the gift she brought me and that it meant more to me, than she could possible imagine.

Now, for a moment, think of the chain of events that occurred that enabled that elderly woman to be a ray of Light to someone. First, the so-called tragedy of our house fire touched a part of the Divine Love within her, which enabled her to act in a loving way to a complete stranger. She had to search through her personal belongings for the item she wanted to give me. And I suspect, she offered her prayers for our family in the privacy of her home or church.

Her small thimble was all that she was able to offer; yet my gratitude was immense. When she left, I cried tears of joy. She was a perfect example of Divine Love in action. When we act upon the inner stirrings of our heart no matter how insignificant we think our loving action might be, we are living from our true nature. Our fire gave that woman the opportunity to experience the meaning and purpose of our lives, **to express unconditional love!**

My own heart was bursting inside as I thought of the moment she would return "home" to be with our Creator and have her life review. I could envision her joy when the scene appears before her of that rainy Spring day when she knocked on my kitchen door and gave me so much more than a tiny thimble. She would understand only at that moment in union with the Light of God that the tiny isolated moment with me was a shining example of her life's purpose. It's like the winner crossing the finish line at the Olympics and shouting, "I did it!" How thrilled she will be to discover that she did it! She loved unconditionally! The light bulb will flash deep within her spiritual consciousness as mine did during my experience. So that's what it's all about!

We don't have to wait until we die before we get that message. We can learn that lesson right now! We need to be guided more by the promptings of our heart rather than our heads if we are to evolve into a state of being that transcends the limited boundaries of selfhood. Faith empowers us to begin the journey in our evolutionary thrust that was and is being Divinely created for us. When we realize that we are composed of the same energy as that of the Light of God, it becomes a very natural and simple process of growth. We can then begin to know at the core of our being that we are one with God and one with the universe. Our connectedness to that truth will eliminate the feeling of separation from God, and we will reflect outwardly from ourselves our own ray of Light that will help illuminate the world's consciousness.

We are all rays of Light, the energy of Divine Love. As such, we find completeness when our Light is radiating outwardly from us into the universe. Every individual has been created to shine its Light into the world. We cannot do this, however, unless we have the consciousness to realize this. For some, this knowledge comes from the intuitive process within. Some are natural born lovers. For many others however, their Light is hidden from their own view as well as from the view of others. Traumatic life experiences, cynicism, defense mechanisms, and fear are some of the many layers of protective disguises utilized by man in order to hide himself from his true self.

Spirit's Voice within us encourages us to become involved with the Divine to help perfect His Creation. We were created with such tender love and concern for us, and we have wonderful things planned for our lives and for those whose lives our ray of Light will touch. The Light will always give us more than we need so that we can share with others in need. The Light within us is indeed mystifying, but rest assured, the Light knows exactly where we are to be led as instruments of the Light's inherent goodness and love. The Light will illuminate our path gently and carefully so that we don't get lost along the way. Spirit's Voice will speak to our soul, gently adjusting our attitudes and purposes. Our view of people and life will gradually be seen the way Spirit sees things. Our own inner Light will reflect dazzling new wonders of compassion, understanding, gentleness, and love that will make Spirit's Presence in humanity so real and discernible.

I am totally convinced that as an individual recognizes one's true self through whatever path of discovery one took, one must then assume the responsibility of enabling us to discover our own true nature as well. The very root of that responsibility is the oneness of Spirit that is seen as love. If we want to live with peace and harmony in our world, each person must begin to contribute their thread in the fabric of our society.

Dear friend, let your Light shine from you at all times. The more Light that you project, the more Light comes through you to help you and others prepare for the wonders ahead. Where there is Light there is peace. Where there is Light there is hope. Where there is Light there is healing. Where there is Light there is truth. Where there is Light there is LOVE.

THE RECOGNITION OF LOVE

We need contrasts to recognize truth. One must be first aware of one's own human imperfection, for then one will be able to realize spiritual perfection in all things outside oneself and within oneself. The ability to recognize one's spiritual perfection is the result of the perceived illusion of separateness. The idea that something is less than perfect is the result of negative thoughts. Remember, while positive energy is the result of love in action, negative energy on the other hand, is the result of fear thoughts, whose intent is to create the illusion of separation. In reality however, there is only love.

Universal laws govern all that the Holy One has created. The energy of pure, perfect love radiates in all directions and is readily accessible to all who lovingly, open their hearts to receive it. The energy of love will always guide and direct one into action that calls to the adherence of universal laws. The resulting action produces harmony and unity in all things. Peace and joy are the reward given to a heart that has been elevated to act from love.

has given us the ability and the right to share in His Creation. When we remember that our dreams and ideals are greater than ourselves, we can also remember that we can tap into the Great Creative Mind that can help us bring out from the depths of our creative consciousness the precious gifts that lie dormant.

Even though we live in a world of matter, our Creator is at work co-creating with us among the tiny particles of protons and electrons, forming, revealing, and evolving. When we have a soul that is consciously and actively working through our physical bodies, the powers with which it is endowed will manifest. On the other hand, however, if the soul is being inhibited by the ego or lower self, which is always anxious to shine and is often mistaken in its estimates of our capacities, it will create limitations to our creative possibilities.

Those individuals who have been able to express their soul's Light through the physical body will never be happy unless they have done what they came into the world to accomplish. You see, the Light's Love within us is like a magnet drawing us closer to our own Light in all its glory and beauty, rendering our personality with graciousness, strength, and unparalleled sincerity. When we truly aspire to furnish the inner conditions needed to receive the wisdom and graces available to us from our Creator, God will never withhold that which we have prepared ourselves to receive. You will grasp that truth only to the degree with which you are ready to understand, no more, no less.

Dear friend, Spirit Consciousness manifests as a gift to you from the Light of God. With all your heart, be willing to let it grow within you, for it is by becoming unified with it that you become a channel for the Light to bring love into the world.

Only the expression of unconditional love brings spiritual perfection and peace.

Divine Love sees no superiority or distinction among persons. It embodies a loving kindness that embraces the welfare of all individuals, its perfection flows at no cost. Those who love without selfishness come into the Presence of God, directing every thought accordingly to manifest perfect peace and harmony.

What we think about love has a direct affect upon our body by the daily thoughts we have. Joy or pain ensues when we love or hate; there is no other alternative. Love is the greatest power in the universe, and it will bring us more happiness than any other means combined. Like an exquisite rose waiting to blossom with its intended God-given potential, the beauty and fragrance of man's life will be determined by the sum total expression of one's ability to live one's life lovingly. One's life, perfumed with its sweet nectar of love, will attract love back to us like a honeybee drawn to the nectar of the flower. **The purpose of life is to LOVE!**

Words of wisdom cannot be challenged for as truth exists, so does the energy that sustains truth, **love.** When the heart is prepared with the Spirit of love, there is no need for proof. Love recognizes love. No words are needed. To prove the existence of love is impossible; it can only be experienced directly. When one is fully ready to embrace it without reservation, to behold the indwelling Spirit of love is to know the God-force within - the spark of life that is the Source of all creation. To know **love** is to know **God.**

Love transcends language, theologies, and doctrines. If we are a loving person, we are a Godly person. Even if we are not affiliated with any particular religious sect or practice any form of spiritual rituals, we will know God for **God is love.** The ray of Light that shines through us at any time that we respond from a loving position is that part of the Divine within us. Spirit asks nothing more of us than learning to live our lives as that ray of Light to others. I beg you, don't underestimate the value of what you might consider a tiny fragment of a loving response and choose not to act upon that response because it isn't "big enough." We do not see the larger picture as Spirit sees it in order that we may see the significance of our actions. But I can promise you, even the smallest act of kindness and compassion, in thought, word, or deed is just as great as the greatest act. It is the same Spirit working through you as Light in the world. Open your heart to those inner loving promptings no matter how great or small your response.

When I think about the elderly woman who brought me the small thimble, I reflect upon the many lives she touched, but she has no knowledge of this. Every time I give a talk, I tell her story, and many people are deeply moved. This book will reach many people and as a result, she will be thought of in a very loving and touching way. It will serve to heighten people's understanding of the meaning and purpose of their own lives, to act upon the still small voice in one's heart and to express unconditional love.

You too, will perhaps never know the effect your love has had upon another in this life, and that's okay. After all, unconditional love means loving without expecting anything in return such as praise, gifts, favors, etc. Humanity can be transformed one individual at a time by learning to be a channel of that ray of Light in the world by assuming individual responsibility. YOURS!

We all want to be loved, yet we think it is human love that we desire. How often we have experienced the love of someone only to be forsaken after a while. We think others will understand us and forgive us our transgressions only to learn they do not. During my life review, I understood that only God understands us. God never abandons us, and we are cherished no matter what we have done. Ask for forgiveness, and God wipes our slate clean.

No, it is not human love that we think we need in order to be made whole. Look no further than in your own heart. Although Divine Love cannot be described, it can be felt as the joy in your heart when you have sufficiently developed your awareness enough to attune your will with Divine Will. Your will becomes a Divine gift that chisels away the conflicts of human life. Look within yourself and make sure that what you see both your good and bad tendencies accurately portray your personality. You know when you are doing something you shouldn't. The feeling you are having is Spirit's Voice within. If you are attuned to Divine Will, you will see that you are awakening your will to choose good instead of evil in every situation because you really desire to do so.

The soul, which is Divine Life and Love, knows exactly what the individual is capable of accomplishing. The loving Voice within will nudge us to act upon an inspiration, and if we accept it, we can be comforted by realization that we are fulfilling the work we were called by the Light to do. How glorious our confidence in Spirit becomes when we know Spirit is working with us to assure the completion of our work. Ineffable Love will console us, and Spirit's Voice will be heard in the peacefulness of our soul bonding us to Spirit in a way nothing else could.

Dear friend, you are Divine Love. Know it, feel it, and be it! Live life as if nothing else matters except love. As you dwell within that love, know that the Light's Love for you is unconditional and limitless. Wear the cloak of love that enfolds and protects you from all troubles, comforting you and bringing you Heavenly Peace!

OUR THOUGHTS CREATE
OUR EXPERIENCE OF REALITY

The Creator created a perfect plan of balance and harmony when our world was created with all things working together for the ultimate good of all. We have all heard the saying, "God doesn't make mistakes," well, that's true. It's *people* who have made the mistakes that have upset the balance and harmony within our world as a result of the way they *chose to think.*

Our thoughts create our experience of reality. Thoughts can either be used constructively to enhance our lives, or thoughts can be used destructively to limit or harm ourselves or others. Let me repeat myself because that point is so important to remember. *Our thoughts create our experience of reality.*

There was a point during my encounter with the Light when I became aware that our physical reality is an illusion and not our true reality, as we perceive it. The real or actual reality is the all-encompassing love I was experiencing to its fullest with the Light. In that spiritual state, there is only love, pure and unconditional. Nothing else real exists. This is the state of perfection that we were created to be. Our thoughts, however, can change our perception of our being, changing that perception from our *true self of Divine Love* to a false self of separation and alienation.

Our purpose as human beings while on this earthly plane is to discover, affirm, and live from our actual preordained reality of pure unconditional love. That love from which God created us is the same love that God IS. That love is constant, unchanging, and eternal. That spiritual part of us is an actual living part of the Divine Presence within us. Everything else is an illusion. This truth became such a profound revelation to me during my experience. I recall thinking how we human beings have limited our perception of reality by accepting only as truth anything that can be observed, tested, or reproduced by scientific methodology.

What I experienced was yet another dimension greater in truth and perception than our physical reality.

There is another part of our existence that is viable at the same time that we are experiencing this observable reality. The other dimension, the intangible non-observable through our physical senses, is the actual, genuine and pure reality. It is the unchanging reality, the spiritual state of being in which the soul knows its true Divine self - Divine Love, and the importance of living one's life from that state of consciousness.

You and I are beings of Divine Love. We are spiritual beings because we originated from our true Source of Being - God. God is Love; therefore, we as co-inheritors are also love. We cannot deny that at the very nature of our being, we are souls of pure Divine Love. God is our spiritual parent, and we are God's children. If God is Love, then we are love, it's as simple as that. The only difficulty you may have in understanding that is that of degree. Take for an example, the sand in the desert. The desert is a vast, enormous place made up of trillions and trillions of grains of sand. Now, if you were to scoop up a handful of that sand, you'll discover that each grain that you are holding in your hand constitutes the same characteristics of the whole desert. There is no difference in the makeup. Each particle of sand resembles the other, and each resembles the whole.

We are the same. God is the whole, and we are the individual segments or parts of it. By nature, we have the very same characteristics as God, and that is love. When we turn to the spirit nature of us and rely on it for all of our answers to our questions, we will always be nurtured lovingly and given the correct guidance to ensure balance, harmony, and peace - the way the universe was created to be.

We are one with the Light of God and one with everyone else in creation. We are perfect souls of Divine, unconditional love. Now ego will scream at us at times and try to dissuade us from thinking this way. The ego will sometimes say, "Hey, wait a minute, that's not true. I'm a terrible person. I'm not worthy of such love." But if you slow down and stop talking to yourself this way and just listen to the inner, still small Voice within, the intuitive, which is Spirit's Voice within, will give you the honest answers.

Ego's voice will always scream and shout at us to try to get us to listen to its perceived truth, but our intuitive Voice will always speak softly, gently, and lovingly. This is the true nature of Divine Love. Tenderly, it hold us to its breast of Love and quietly affirms and honors our true being. That still, small voice within us knows our true reality, our perfection, and our oneness with the universe and one with Divine Love. There is something deep down within us that knows the truth, and it knows that it **knows!** Unfortunately, because the ego's voice is often times so loud, we pay more attention to it than to the true Voice of Love, the Holy Presence within.

During my experience, I was shown that the ego is the world's voice and that it will always try to guide us into making choices that will prove through our experiences that the world is right. It must somehow strengthen our beliefs that we're right, they're wrong, and they're to blame and so on. It tries to manipulate us into making choices that lead us toward conflict and sepa-rateness. But the true voice, the Holy Spirit by its very nature, cannot deceive, and it cannot counsel us with choices that will lead us to any other reality other than love, oneness, harmony, and peace.

I'm suggesting that in order to be the fullest expression of the loving person who we already are, we need to change our thoughts and direct them away from being a servant of the world's purpose and direct them to being a servant of **love**. Thereby, we become a co-creator of truth with the Divine Presence within us. Spirit will always teach love because that is what God **IS**. There is absolutely no unloving characteristic associated with our Creator.

Our task in this life is to remove the veil of illusion that we choose to hold to ourselves by eliminating negative thought forms that mask our true identity. In short, we have to return "home" to our true spiritual nature and allow the Light of God to self-express Himself in and through us. Why? Because only when we live from a loving response can we fulfill our intended purpose of our soul housed in this physical body of ours. Only when we live from a loving response do we draw back to us a life filled with love, purpose, joy, and peace.

If someone else had told you that they have a low opinion of you, and you are to blame for other's misfortunes, you are holding immobilizing guilt feelings toward yourself. You have bought into the illusion that you are not a loving being. Holding onto that illusion as part of your belief system will only draw negative experiences to you that will reinforce those negative thoughts. Okay, I hear you. You say, "I've had a rough time of life, someone did this and that to me. I can't help myself, this is the way I am, and I can't change things."

Although it's true you may not be able to change people or situations and those things that are not conducive to your physical or mental good, you **can** change your perception and find meaning in that experience. That change in perception is the key that will unlock your life from one of mental slavery to one of freedom to live lovingly according to the natural law of the universe.

Every day is a new beginning; the past is already gone. You can't bring it back, and the future is promised to no one. The only thing you have is the present moment, right now. So choose from your conscious, mental thoughts to let go of all the past hurts, disappointments, fear, and guilt. You will then begin to discover the beautiful human being that you truly are.

Sorrow is found throughout every human experience. All around us are the sick, the dying, the lonely, the suffering. In far too many depressed minds, the thought arises that one would be "better off" by committing suicide, especially when being told there is a glorious afterlife awaiting all of us at the moment of our physical death. The **first** thing that would occur would be an encounter with the Light of God and subsequent life review. I state this based upon the knowledge that I received during my own personal encounter with the Light of God. This knowledge is also backed up by the millions of persons worldwide who have had a near-death experience and who similarly agree, that earthly life must be used to its fullest to extend **love** outwardly from ourselves to others, to learn who we are, and why we are here.

When that soul arrives at that Transcendent Reality upon a person's death, he/she will fully understand the spiritual implications regarding the act of suicide, whether that act stemmed from depression, hopelessness, or any other reason. It is the first time that one fully realizes the meaning of life! It's too late at that point to say, "Oh gee, now I get the picture. Can I go back and try again? Some do return to the physical realm as evidenced by the numbers of near-death experiencers who returned. Many however, stay on the other side. I feel so deeply compelled to urge everyone to listen to what individuals are proclaiming upon their return to this physical reality. We have been there, and we have returned to help others elevate their spiritual consciousness while life upon this earth is being lived so that humanity can evolve toward our intended destiny. However, people who have killed themselves by suicide are not punished for it by our Creator. They experience the same unconditional love from our Creator as someone who didn't commit suicide. The Creator doesn't judge us, we judge ourselves and we can be pretty hard on ourselves when during our life review, we fully understand the meaning of life.

Each individual life plays a profound role in creating that destiny, no matter what tragic circumstances befall us or how helpless or hopeless our situation. We may not understand this while inhabiting our physical body, but certainly we will understand it when our spiritual body is manifested in the spiritual realm. When our spiritual body is revealed to us, our spiritual awareness becomes truth itself, and the reality of that truth is overwhelming! Believe me!

Sorrow of any kind is not akin to leading the kind of spiritual life that the soul within us seeks. Our thoughts create our experience of reality. When we are living in our physical body, our awareness is often governed by our false or ego self which chooses paths often leading to heartache and sorrow. Human error is always the culprit of sorrow whether it is errors of judgment, excessive self-indulgence, rebellion, apathy, or pride. All disease is *dis-ease*, a lack of harmonious balance between a living organism and its environments. All too often, we want to attach blame to the condition or tragedy that causes our sorrow. But in reality, that is not the problem. The real problem is our **reaction** to that condition.

Dear friend, all power to clear your mind and transform your consciousness from fear, lack, and limitation is within you. Spirit's Loving Voice will gently lead the way, aligning your thoughts toward love, forgiveness, and healing. Wherever you go, whatever you do, be consciously aware that the Light of God is with you in every situation. Release the judgments and preconceived ideas you hold of how life should be and surrender instead to your intuitive loving voice that will lift you into the Light of Peace.

THE REAL YOU

As long as we are focusing our attention on people or items in our outer world to provide for our happiness, we will always feel frustrated because we simply cannot find it "out there." Turning inwardly toward ourselves will bring about the transforming power of the spiritual joy within us. Jesus said, *"The kingdom of God is within you."* (Luke 17:21) The first thing we must do to discover true happiness is to believe those words from Jesus' teachings. If you can't do that, I would suggest that you carefully evaluate how much or how little faith you do have in that statement, for just a tiny mustard seed's worth is all we need. It will grow, it will expand, and it will increase. The important concept is to have *some amount of faith* through your conscious desire to seek the happiness you crave. Intuitively, you will begin to become aware of things you need to do to nourish the small amount of faith you do have. Trust that all of the answers to all of your problems, anxieties, and unhappiness lay within you.

The next step is to become aware of your intuition, which is the gateway to the soul. It's that still small Voice within that often times, we just don't listen to. We've been conditioned by society to disregard intuitive messages as not being valid in some way. We've been conditioned to pay less attention to ourselves and to our own beliefs.

It isn't necessary to understand everything that happens to us. Often times, we struggle to understand something, and in the process we become even more confused. When we cease to struggle to understand, then we know without understanding. When we reach that point of understanding intuitively, we are in perfect harmony with our Divinity which needs no understanding, only acceptance. At that stage, you'll be like a leaf floating on a vast river flowing effortlessly on its journey under the river's power and in the same way, your love will flow unrestrained.

That part of us is being guided by a higher spiritual power that we humans are incapable of understanding. We have compulsively concealed our loving nature through habit and reacting to circumstances in our lives. Once we understand that our very basic nature is oneness with the Divine, and that we are pure beings of that same love, the next logical step is to eliminate the circumstances that conceal our basic loving nature. They are the features that are the opposite of love: hate, anger, temptation, jealousy, or any feeling that hides or covers up the loving spiritual being that we are.

If I asked you to describe all the characteristics of what you thought God to be, what would you say? I'll mention a few, and then you can add more of your own concepts. I could say that God is loving, compassionate, forgiving, wise, helpful, patient, and trusting. Those qualities are positive and righteous. Remember, we have the same attributes as God at the core of our being. If we eliminate the negative reactions to situations in our lives, we should automatically eliminate the circumstances that feed into our lives, which brings us the unhappiness that dominates us. Love flows through automatically when we remove the negativity in our lives. We don't have to act more lovingly, we just need to remove the negative emotions we have. Love automatically comes forth.

There is a beautiful Biblical passage from 1 Corinthians 13:4 that Paul discusses. *"Love is very patient and kind, never jealous or envious, never boastful or proud."* What Paul is saying is that if we eliminate a jealous or boastful reaction to a given situation, we automatically express love. Paul goes on to say, *"Love does not seek its own way."* Again, if you work to get rid of the emotion of arrogance, the very nature of your loving being comes forth. "Love does not seek its own way." Again, if you work to get rid of the emotion of arrogance, the very nature of your loving being comes forth. *"It is not irritable or touchy. It does not hold grudges and will hardly even notice when others do it wrong."*

Obviously, there are many times when we get irritable at our children, spouse, boss, or neighbor for some irritating behavior against us. We may even justify our anger by saying, "Well, who wouldn't be angry!" I'm not suggesting for one moment that we should repress our emotions for even Jesus at times became angry and frustrated. The important item to remember is first to acknowledge the negative feeling, then take corrective measures to dissipate it so it doesn't continue to have a negative effect upon you.

This negative effect is detrimental to your health and sense of well-being. Consider for a moment what happens when negative emotions govern your consciousness. Your physical body becomes tense, depressed, and tired. You may even experience illness, headaches, ulcers, and respiratory problems. You may also become critical, vindictive, or volatile. In short, you become a very unloving person.

If you can't love others, at least don't hurt them. No one is expecting us to be perfect human beings. I'm not, you're not, and neither is the other person. What each person is, is a struggling, fumbling human being, trying to do the best we can under the given circumstances at the given moment.

Love is learned. The earliest teachers we had were our parents. Perhaps one of the mistakes we made was placing unrealistic expectations upon them as our teachers. We expect them to be perfect and have the correct advice for us when we're uncertain or confused. We may never realize that they too were struggling, fumbling human beings, and struggling to do the best they could under the given circumstances at that time. No one ever taught our parents the right or wrong way to love. There was no university or school to learn it. They had never been parents before. How could they possibly teach you, their child, all the lessons they learned as parents. You were their classroom where they learned the lessons of parenting. They can only draw upon the experience of their own parental teachings. But then again we ask, who taught them? Who taught them before them?

My point is that there is no place where we can learn to become fully accepting, non-condescending, all-embracing human beings. We do the best we can with the tools we have at the time. In the process, we may not have learned how to love very well. Unless we have that love for ourselves initially, and we are able to accept and forgive ourselves, we cannot give that love to others. We become blocked. Our inner self is constipated, and unless we take a spiritual laxative to free our selves from bottled up self-hatred and learn to love, we are always going to be in that state of constipated emotion of self-hatred and no fulfillment.

If it's not possible for you to have the desire to be a more loving person and to learn all you can about the process of self-discovery, that marvelous God-given gift of uniqueness, then I would ask that through the course of your life, if you cannot become a loving person by choice, at least don't hurt anyone else intentionally. If you can't love them, don't hurt them. They are doing the best they can as human beings traveling down life's difficult road, and they may not live up to your expectations.

The hurts, especially intentionally directed toward someone, usually have lasting effects. They burn. They scar. Many people cannot recover from those scars. Through our careless words of anger and frustration, we project unloving negative energy out toward others, giving them an opportunity to choose and accept that energy to themselves. We are all like vast sponges absorbing into our consciousness everything that is said and unsaid. Our self-image is molded to a great part by the way others treat us. If I fail to live up to your expectations, can you just see me as someone who momentarily stumbled and made a stupid mistake? Instead of yelling and screaming at me or getting even with me in some retaliative way, can you just reach out to me and hold out your hand so that I can grasp it and pick myself up again? Can you just put a Band-Aid on my bruised ego and send me on my way? I'm not asking for a lecture. I just fell down, and I hurt. All that I'm asking is your hand so I can stand up and be on my way again. When you reach outwardly from a loving response in this way, your own self-image will take a giant step forward because you chose to respond lovingly. Sometimes all we need when we're making a mess of things is to reach out and find a waiting hand on which to hold. We'll be fine then. We don't need a lot of reassurance or a lot of patronizing words, but we just need a Band-Aid. At times we feel at a loss for words when someone is hurting so our tendency is to withdraw because we don't know what to do to help that person. We don't know how to love, so we don't do anything. Perhaps we need to remind ourselves at that time that the most that we may be capable of giving is our hand and a Band-Aid. That may have been all that person needed.

If people let you down, lift them up into your heart. You may not be able to solve their problems for them or offer them words of wisdom, but if you become insensitive or callused toward someone who failed to live up to your expectations, you become the loser. You lose a part of your humanness that you can reach out and touch others. Remember, if someone disappoints you, they don't need your wrath or cynicism, they need a Band-Aid sprinkled with some of your forgiveness to help heal their transgressions.

If you simply cannot find it in your heart to forgive someone, bite your lip and don't hurt them. Chances are they already sense your intolerance so why rub salt into their wounds to make them feel worse than they already do. If you can't love them, don't hurt them. Just send them along their way without a lot of extra wounds to nurse. Give up the temptation to criticize them and say words that will pierce their hearts like a double-edged sword. You may be in their position one day. How do you suppose it might feel to be in their shoes? So watch what you say. Does it have the potential to hurt someone? If it does, it is better to say nothing than to deliberately hurt someone. Anytime you feel that human beings just aren't worth the effort of simple kindness and tolerance, just remind yourself that you too are a member of the human race, and it's pretty nice when someone overlooks your imperfections and allows you to have another chance. No one is asking you to become a totally forgiving, accepting human being if that is not within your means at this time. What I am asking is this: if you can't love others at least don't hurt them. Remember that when you have your life review as I did, you will see the times in your life when you had opportunities to express your loving self to others and didn't. This is a very, very painful life review process so I urge you to use the opportunities that come your way to lessen this painful life review. Remember, we are here to learn how to love unconditionally.

The universe is constructed to work in perfect balance and harmony through the energy of love. The Creator knew how to create us in such a way to alarm us when we are out of balance and not acting from loving responses. Instead of trying to **act** lovingly all the time, try turning your attention away from inwardly responding negatively to situations or relationships that trigger those emotions of anger or any other negative emotion you may be feeling at that moment. Let me give you an example. Let's say you are driving your car on the highway and you have to be at work soon. Someone ahead of you is driving very slowly. As a result, all the traffic is being slowed, and you begin to fear you'll be late for work. You feel yourself welling up with impatience and anger; your teeth start to grind, and mentally you begin fuming at the person ahead of you who is driving too slowly. Your mental thoughts are projecting unspeakable words which I won't dare write in this book. What you have done is mentally and physically worked yourself into a state of anger, anxiety, and a state of un-love. When you finally reach your destination, you still feel tied up in knots and as a result, you are curt in your responses with your co-workers.

Now, let's recreate this scenario. Someone is driving too slowly ahead of you on the highway. You begin to feel those feelings of tension and anger welling up inside of you. The first thing you should do is become *aware* of those feelings. Admit to yourself that mentally, you are feeling some rather unloving feelings toward that individual. This is the critical moment in which you have total control over what happens from this moment on. You can choose to allow the power of those negative emotions to control and dominate you, or you can choose to terminate or abort them.

You can choose to cast those negative feelings aside so that you emerge from that situation feeling relaxed and at peace. You begin by telling yourself to relax. What you are telling your body while it is in this heightened state of anxiety is that you are in control in this situation instead of the situation in control of you. Say the words, "Relax, calm down." Take a deep breath and allow the negative feelings to flow out of you. As you begin to focus on the slow driver in front of you and the inconvenience he is causing you, realize that the individual may have a very good reason for traveling slowly at that time. You have no idea who that person is or what his needs are. Perhaps he is on some medication and needs to drive with more caution. Perhaps he is tired and is concerned about his safety and **yours** as well.

Whatever the case, just trust that whatever reason he may have for driving slowly, it is a good reason for **him**. So instead of becoming angry with him, it is possible to view him as a caring individual doing the best he can given the circumstances he is confronting at that particular moment. By getting rid of the negative feeling toward that individual, you have opened the door to allow the loving being that you are to come through. Instead of placing the emphasis upon the negative reaction, try placing the emphasis upon being loving simply by allowing the love response within you to flow through you automatically.

That response comes automatically once you nip in the bud, those negative feelings of anger. Let's put it another way. By nature, you are a loving being. This is the same constituent as the Light of God within you. When through your free will you choose to react to a given situation in an unloving way, you become an unloving person. But, if you catch yourself beginning to recognize those unloving responses and nip it in the bud, you can abort those feelings and when you do, you revert back to your natural, normal state of being -love. It's just that simple.

If you react to situations in an unloving way and justify it by calling it a loving reaction, it will always and clearly, reveal its truth to you. When it truly is a loving response, it will reward you with assured peace, contentment, and balance. No matter how hard you try to deceive yourself into believing you acted in a loving way, if it doesn't leave behind that real feeling of peace, contentment, and joy, then you are not acting in a loving way. It is time to re-evaluate your response. Were you acting that way because of some selfish desire on your part? Were you trying to manipulate someone into doing something you wanted?

Love will always seek to build, not destroy. Love will always seek to bring about the ultimate good for the individual for whom it is offered. Love will never attack the self-esteem of another person. Love is always flawless and uplifting. It will bring order out of chaos. When you live your life lovingly, you will feel that life is a beautiful flower garden blooming so profusely and oh, so fragrantly. Joy and serenity will replace the tension and frustration with which you previously lived. You will become more patient and gentle. Your problems will be much easier to handle because you will become sensitive to the healing power that a loving response emits.

No matter how aberrant or tragic the circumstance, you will become like a willow tree, able to bend, to give, and to receive. The inner Light of Divine or pure Love will begin to radiate from within you. Your eyes will begin to take on a new expression of softness and sparkle. It is said that the "eyes are the windows to the soul." People will sense something radiating from you, and they will be drawn to you and desire to be with you. Love will always seek to be self-expressed. God always seeks your ultimate good. Your purpose as a human being is to grow in love and to allow the Light of God within you to be expressed through you. When we are in the Light's Presence one day, we will not be judged by the wealth we were able to accumulate or the position on the corporate ladder that we attained, but rather, by the amount of love we self-express through our hearts and in our lives. **This is the fundamental message the Light wanted me to promulgate to others!**

You will know the inner joy of the Light within you as the Light intimately reveals the Divine message of love through you. This love will nurture and care for you just as a mother tenderly cares for her child. With utmost assurance you will know that only a loving nature will bring you the authentic happiness which you are seeking in your life. You will discover that *"the kingdom of God is within you."* is not a theological concept, but rather, the **actual presence of God dwelling within you and radiating His Love from you.**

Precious opportunities are presented to us each day to allow us to respond from our true loving selves. Cherish those moments when someone touches your life in some way, and then seize the opportunity to convey your gratitude to him or her. One chilly, rainy April morning, a local nursery hosted a horticulture symposium complete with lecture, demonstrations, and exhibits on various home gardening topics. Being an avid gardener, rain, sleet or snow would not keep me from attending this informative symposium.

When I arrived, the nursery was bustling with people, all anticipating the approaching gardening season. Their shopping carts began to fill up with all sorts of perennial flowers, peat moss, seeds, and assorted tools and plant containers. Radiant smiles from the gardening enthusiasts beamed like sunshine amidst the dreary chilly rain pouring from the clouds overhead. After spending a half-day learning new gardening techniques, new plant cultivars, and chatting with other gardening devotees, I decided it was time to leave. As I was walking past some of the plants positioned carefully around the display tables indoors, I heard a lovely musical sound. Following the melodic sound, I discovered seated in the corner in the rear of the cactus isle, a lovely woman dressed in a beautiful white long flowing dress playing the most exquisite angelic-like music on her harp. Her beautiful music was being played as background music for the shoppers.

Slowly approaching the woman, I noticed that I was the only person who stopped and listened to her play her ethereal music on her instrument. I stood before her transfixed and seemingly lost in the moments of awe as the music ebbed from her harp and gently washed over my entire being. Her eye caught mine, and she smiled warmly at me, surprised that someone stood before her and was actually and intently listening to her music. I returned the smile as I watched her brow rising and lowering as her graceful fingertips plucked at each string as if to personally accompany each high and low note on its journey into the atmosphere.

I felt the warm trickle of a teardrop gently touching my cheek, responding to the ineffable joy her music was bringing me. When she finished playing, I seized the opportunity to approach her and said, "I have to tell you that your music moved me to tears. You play from the heart of your soul, and you have touched me very deeply today. You have a very special gift, and I want to thank you very much for sharing that gift with me." With a gasp, she clenched her hand over her heart and a tear fell from her eye. "Oh my goodness," she cried, "Thank you so much for telling me that. It means so much to me that someone would actually come up and say that to me."

For the next ten seconds, we stood speechless, staring into each other's tear-filled eyes. Words at that point were needless. Our hearts understood the language that connected our humanness. We had joined in a moment of oneness as we both expressed genuine gratitude for one another's impact on our spirits. Her gifted music had touched my soul, and my kind words had touched hers. We both left behind a part of ourselves that honored our true Divine Nature, and we both emerged from that encounter feeling that our presence in this world has meaning and purpose, even in the most common of circumstances.

When you are expressing the true loving being you are, your motives will always be honorable and correct, and your self-image will be enhanced. When others seek to take advantage of you or try to manipulate you, intuitively you will know that it would be wrong to submit to an unloving action based upon someone else's unloving response to you. You will begin to take corrective action toward someone who is harmful to you. Your love will enable you to become a more responsible person. Corrective action will be taken from a calm and inner-directed basis instead of from an unloving perspective like anger or retaliation. As a result, this will lead to inner peace and resolution saving both you and the other person a lot of negative emotionally charged strain.

Remember that the logic behind expressing love instead of un-love is that you are naturally expressing the **real you**, the God-given gift of Divine Light and Divine Love. You must decide if you wish to take affirmative action to change if you are responding from an unloving nature. Habits are very difficult to change. Some of your deeply rooted habitual ways of reacting to outer circumstances are firmly implanted in your consciousness. It's easier to revert back to the usual ways of responding to your outer life situations. It's a lot easier to say, "I'm going to get even with him." Resist that temptation, please.

After you have identified your negative feeling, remember to acknowledge that feeling, don't try to deny that feeling. Then act to take corrective measures to change or dissipate that emotion. When that happens, you do not give power to negative energy. You choose to give that power to the positive energy of love. The more you relinquish the destructive power of negative responses in your life and choose to respond from a positive, constructive reaction of love, the more you will reap the benefits of a healthier forever in your consciousness no matter what happens to you even when there will be moments when your heart is paralyzed by fear thoughts, and it is impossible to think right thoughts. As you recall, I was in that predicament when I thought God no longer loved me because I was intentionally going to marry a non-Catholic. The truth that the Light of God revealed to me is this: God's mission is to love us unconditionally and for eternity, to be aware of our slightest cry, and to help us.

The next part is very important for you to understand. The reason so many of us feel that God is not doing anything to help us is that we do not recognize Spirit's Indwelling Power to help us when called upon. This part is crucial for you to understand. When we acknowledge and trust Spirit with the absolute conviction that only God and not human efforts will bring about the healing of our sorrows, only then will Spirit become manifest.

In my case, I am sure that by Divine Grace this knowledge was revealed to me so that I would pass it on, so others would be transformed just as I had been. My advice is: If you want to take a short cut on the path to Truth, go directly to the Source of Truth promised to dwell within us. You will be seeking Truth that will come through direct revelation in your own soul. You will hear His Voice flowing through you in unlimited degree because no matter how insignificant you think you are in this world, Spirit cherishes you! Spirit is always trying to be revealed to you so that you will be more comfortable and happy. Listen!

Have you ever wondered about the desires of your heart, where they come from and what they mean? If you desire good and not evil, you are actually longing for more of the Divine, who is the substance of infinite supply waiting to come forth into manifestation. Spirit initiates the process of desiring something for us, and then our hearts are nudged with Spirit's still small Voice to bring that desire up to our consciousness. We would never have had the thought in the first place. Delight in the goodness of our Creator's Love for us in helping us to become all that we were created to be. Kindled by the inner Light of Love, there is no external condition in the entire universe that can hold back the Light's infinite tenderness in bringing us our intended good.

To bring the Light's desires for us into manifestation, each of us must come to a point when we no longer seek help from outside sources, but instead with our whole being we must desire that our Divine Selves be revealed to us personally within us. I can promise you that when you ask for this revelation to be made known to you, you have direct access to Divine Truth. Forget about acquiring Truth from books and teachers for intellectual perception can often times be flawed. You must learn first-hand from the One who loves you and who longs to reveal Divine Truth to you **personally**.

Call upon the Light of God in your deepest moments of solitude and prayer and ask to hear His Voice deep within your intuitive self. Have patience for the Holy One wants to be sure that you are absolutely earnest in your desire to commune with Divine Source. As your desire to abide in God is of absolute mental humility, God will be revealed, and His Voice will guide you into wisdom that will transcend your own. From personal experience in the years following my near-death-like experience, I promise that what I have revealed to you is the Light's promise to you. Intellectually, I am relaying this Truth to you, but you must discover for yourself that it works!

Spend quiet time drawing near to God as often as you can. Center your thoughts upon your love for God. Quietly stirring within you will be a feeling of peace. Be in the peace and be still for you need do nothing more. As your intuitive feeling leads you to ask God for something, let the emotion of your heart express your desire and ask always that you will receive that which will be in accordance with your highest good. Remember, you are speaking to the One who loves you more than anyone else in your life! The Light's Love for you will always bring your highest good into manifestation in and through you. The answers to your requests may differ from your expectations, but if you sincerely want Divine Grace be revealed to you, then you will see transformations occurring that move you into a fuller and more beautiful life because it is what Divine Life is meant to be. Without effort on your part, God will manifest Himself through you in Divine appointed time. Be patient and let Divine Grace be done. In time, you will see that the transitions in your life do not need to be feared for if you choose to hang on to the familiar no matter how secure you may feel with it, you may be postponing the day when your fullest, highest gift appears.

In my garden, I am constantly reminded of the abundance our Creator provides as I tend to the beautiful flowers that grow for my enjoyment. In the Spring, I planted one flower plant called Cleome. A rather tall plant, it's spider-like flower heads hovered pompously above the low-growing flowers to give a balanced effect in my flower garden. At the end of the growing season, the entire plant died as expected since its life cycle endures for only one summer. The following Spring, I discovered hundreds of new seedling plants springing up from the soil where the Cleome had thrived the previous year, an abundance that the Creator had pre-determined to provide for as a characteristic in this particular flower plant. The Creator had chosen other plants to have different features such as the rare endangered Indonesian plant, titan arum or "corpse flower," the world's largest flower. The blossom can measure up to four feet and blooms only two or three times during its forty-year life span. The blossom lasts only a few days before collapsing under its own weight. When it does bloom, it releases an offensive odor described as "rotting flesh." This smell attracts beetles, which pollinate the flowers in the wild. During the rare times when it is in bloom, thousands of people are drawn to it hoping to catch a glimpse of this remarkable and unusual plant once during their lifetime. You see, even a flower plant listens to His Voice within to bring about its intended fruition and individuality!

Each of us is a unique individual flower in the garden of God's Heart, and the beauty of our individualism is ours alone to cultivate. God has chosen you to be a magnificent but much different flower than He created for others. Some of us will be considered odd to others but so what! It is the same Divine Life-force ebbing through us that will bring our unique special gifts to fruition to better our world. When you accept that fact, you will get a better sense of your own inherent possibilities. Affirm your own individuality and boldly follow it even if it makes you different from others. That difference is the Divine Plan, and if you allow it to grow and flower as the Creator intends, then the seasons of your life will be abundant with life, and you will cultivate the feeling of being Divinely possessed rather than being self-possessed. You will stand confidently next to others in the flower garden of your life knowing with certainty that the Divine Life-force within is providing you with all you need to reach your inherited potential.

Keep in mind however, you do not need to wilt in the presence of others whose personality is stronger or more intimidating than yours. Personality is human, but individuality is Divine. Personality is governed mainly by ego and listening to voices outside oneself for personal identity. Strive always to remain an individual and let your real self be the sweet fragrance of the flower the Light of God has chosen you to be.

Dear friend, as you experience the gift of life itself, be yourself - the self that comes from the Divine. Your mission on earth is needed and is part of the Divine Grace the Holy One gave you to fulfill. Love chose to express itself to you through your remarkable individual self. Divine Love will never judge, criticize, or punish you. Always, you are loved! Be ecstatic that God is working through you, and all will be well.

CHAPTER 14

THE CALL TO HEAR HIS VOICE

The higher our sights, the better our fate.

The calling I received from the Light of God that miraculous day in 1979 was in essence, a calling **for all of us to hear His Voice** so that we may ascend toward an awareness that the Light enfolds humanity with love. We are being called to love, to forgive, to heal, and to lift ourselves out of the darkness into the Light through the miracle of Divine Grace. We are to remember who we truly are - Divine expressions of God.

In society, people claiming to have had spiritual experiences tend not to tell anyone about them for fear of being labeled as some kind of a nut or religious fanatic. They fear being laughed at and are afraid to show they are different from others. Afraid to reveal the inspirations that lie hidden in their hearts, these people quietly live among us, placing their greatest faith in that which they know as real from their own experience. If they only knew how important it is to ignore the ridicule and release the pent-up innate powers within them, they would be a great advantage to others spiritual growth. Our souls know exactly what we are capable of accomplishing. Whenever an inspiration arises and if we accept it, it can change our lives completely. If we push it away, we may lose a great opportunity to empower others and ourselves. We must all unite and move forward together, sharing our individual callings with the wisdom and love given to us by Spirit. The greater the number of people who bring Spirit awareness into the world, the greater the flow of the Infinite Goodness of God comes onto the earth.

What is a miracle and how do we differentiate it from magic and illusions? The definition in Webster's Dictionary states that a miracle is "an event or effect in the physical world deviating from the known laws of nature, or transcending our knowledge of these laws." It is, therefore, a supernatural event where the laws of nature are temporarily suspended. A true miracle is Holy, has meaning, and comes from God. We all have read about the marvelous miracles documented in the Bible. These signs and wonders always fulfilled a purpose, and that purpose was to affirm God's Love and authority. The swift, powerful intervention by God could not be mistaken for trickery or mistaken for coincidence. Always, miracles are callings that change lives and lift human hearts closer to God.

"Ok," you might say, "Those miracles happened thousands of years ago during Biblical times and during the time when Jesus was alive. What about today? We live in a technically-advanced age. Do miracles still occur?" My answer is a resounding yes! In Hebrews 13:8, it is written, *"Jesus Christ is the same yesterday, today, and forever."* The Divine powers of God have never left us, reminding us that God's Love is always near to strengthen our faith and lift our hearts closer to the Divine Presence within.

Certainly, my experiences with the Light of God are miracles in my opinion. One need only look at my life and the fruits of my Spirit following my experiences to know that something extraordinary happened that cannot be explained by chance. The results are visible even after many years have passed. There have been attempts by science to explain the type of experience I had by attributing it simply to brain function. I cannot disagree more. Brain is finite, Spirit is infinite. What I experienced with the Light of God is beyond science and reductionism. Anyone trying to reduce Spirit into logical components that can be intellectually understood by science is barking up the wrong tree.

What is so awesome about miracles is that it shows us that God is alive and that God is with us in our midst in these modern times with a willingness to intervene in our lives by showing us Divine Love. One way to discern if a miracle has occurred is to look for the meaning behind the miracle. God demonstrates Grace, Wisdom, and Love and personal involvement in our lives when miracles are performed. Hearing God's Voice within is surely a miracle, so listen for it.

The Holy One calls each and every one of us to hear His Voice so that we are elevated above our lesser resources to build a more stable foundation to comprehend the real and inner meaning to our lives. We recognize the truth that emerges from the Voice within without having to reason it out. From this wisdom, we bring about our part of the Divine Plan to bring into our world a radiant personality, filled with spiritual grace that makes life worth living.

Spirit's Voice within us has already been put in place. It is not something we have to wish or hope that we can be blessed with. Spirit's Voice is silent until we invite Our Great Teacher to speak to us. God has chosen us to hear His Voice within and to enjoy intimacy with Him. All we have to do is to know with certainty that we are cherished and that we are being called to become Holy instruments of the Light's Precious Love. Again, may I remind you that the wisdom you are reading in this book stemmed from the vast knowledge my Great Teacher was pouring into my consciousness when I was merged into oneness with the Light of God. I never received any formal theological teachings prior to my experience. I was basically, a blank slate for the wisdom which my Great Teacher chose to inscribe into my consciousness that I was instructed to share with others. It is my sincere hope that this book reveals that wisdom to you for and happier life. Remember, the natural loving person that you already are will automatically come through when you abort the negative response to any situation.

Although it may take time to change old habits, we are capable of self-improvement if we are motivated to do so. As you begin to peel away the layers of negatively charged reactions to your outer world situations, you will begin to create inwardly and outwardly, your true being. Blessed will be the many individuals who pass through your life for they will have known the **real you**. As you begin your journey of self-realization, first comes the faith that by nature, you are a loving person. Remember also that just a small mustard seed's amount of faith is all that is needed. Seek always to be guided from within for the Light of God resides there. Let the Light's Voice nurture and guide you. You are loved beyond human comprehension!

A transformed life emerges as you grow in love. Respond not with negativity but rather, by allowing the true nature of your being to automatically flow. It will bless you and others as well, but above all, it will glorify God as you fulfill the purpose of your creation - to live lovingly.

Dear friend, you are one with the Light of God. Realize this, love this and share this. You are the temple of the Holy Spirit. Know the truth about yourself and be the Love of God. Spirit's Voice within will whisper this truth to you so that you are lifted into an expanded awareness of your Divine Nature and your oneness with the Holy One. Let pure trust in His Voice within guide you to new levels of truth.

DIVINE GRACE

I want to tell you about a profound truth I received during my encounter with the Light of God. It is so imperative that you digest this truth within your entire being and let it dwell this is the reason that I was sent back from Heaven's door to the physical dimension.

The call to hear His Voice will illuminate our minds as the Light of Truth begins to illumine our understanding of any past, present, or future situation. Our Divine destinies await us with a timeless power as close to us as our next heartbeat. His Voice is constantly revealing inner secrets to us but unless we have learned to open ourselves up to receive the higher realization, His Voice cannot reach our mind. His Voice can direct us into the future or the past. There is no limit to the assistance that we can receive from the Divine Presence within us when we seek that help.

My friends, the people who complain that they are unable to hear the Divine Voice within have not convinced themselves that they can hear His Voice. The degree of our faith measures our degree of blessings we receive. God always responds to faith in Him! *"All things whatsoever ye pray and ask for, believe that ye receive them, and ye shall have them."* (Mark 11:24) Trust your soul to bring you Light and Wisdom if you really desire to hear His Voice.

If you want to learn how to receive the God-given lucidity in which the truth is seen and inwardly comprehended, just ASK! Before falling asleep, just whisper softly: "Give me an answer to my concern which will be for my highest good." In this way you can contact wisdom without the interference of the dense fog of the ego that we know is fallible and imperfect. Those who receive revelations of wisdom know beyond a shadow of a doubt that the Voice of God whispered to us, "this is true, this is true!" Lucidity is realized because we were ready to comprehend, or we would never receive this great gift.

In order to invite Divine intervention in our lives, God will not intervene if we cling to our ego's point of view. Remember, ego is riddled with judgment and from the spiritual point of view, the ego's voice must be silenced or transcended, so that Spirit's Voice of non-judgmental unconditional love can be heard.

Because we want to judge others and feel they deserve to suffer for what they have done to us, we naturally assume God wants to punish us for our own shortcomings. The more we judge others, the more we fear judgment from God. The result is fear and separation. No longer will we have the desire to judge one another and inflate our ego's need to feel special. When we experience a consciousness of detachment and a willingness to accept reality on its own terms, human misery ceases, and our physical experiences become arranged as if an invisible hand lovingly supplied a happy outcome for our needs.

The result of heeding the inner guidance of His Voice within is that the needs in our physical world become arranged in such a way so as to bring forth what is intended for our highest good. God will not undo the problems that we choose to hold steadfast to our being because of our attitudes and false beliefs. God will not interfere with our free will. God will, however, encourage us to change our thoughts about our circumstances through our conscience and intuition as we are guided to think about something in a different way that we would not have ordinarily considered.

Our Great Teacher is willing to speak to us and advise us but are we willing to accept the advice that is offered? We have to be very discerning once we have heard His Voice. All too often the ego steps up to the mound and insists on throwing us a curve ball in an attempt to interfere with our spiritual growth. The ego will give us plenty of reasons why we should continue to view our situation through a distorted viewpoint. If any thoughts surface that call you or others to experience guilt, superiority, humiliation, or punishment, you can be assured, it is not the Voice of God within.

You can say that Spirit's Voice can be heard as our conscience which teaches us right from wrong. Instinctively, we know this as our internal guide for living good, moral lives. A popular saying today is: *"What would Jesus do?"* The answer to that question is that our conscience would rightfully lead us to respond to any situation in a loving way.

Through intuition, we can hear the internal Voice bringing us information and guidance that directs us to surprising solutions. History is full of examples of individuals who either were asleep or who were deeply, mentally relaxed when solutions to problems or creativity suddenly appeared. I can vouch for this personally while working on this book. Many times, I was abruptly awakened at three o'clock in the morning with words pouring out of my sleepy consciousness. Immediately, I would get out of bed and transcribe the words into my computer so I wouldn't forget them. A large part of this book was manifest in this way, showing me that Spirit's Voice could be heard even while my sleepy brain was not fully awake. As I responded to God's call in this way by choosing to get out of bed and go to my computer, my Great Teacher was able to help me write this book by detouring my ego and bringing me the help I asked for.

You can recognize Spirit's Voice by the calm, loving, and constructive guidance that comes to you. Peace will always follow wisdom that comes from Spirit. Remember, you have free will, and you always have the choice to write the script of your own life. If you follow the call toward guidance from within, His Voice will always lead you in the right direction, out of the darkness, into the Light.

There is no limit to the countless gifts being brought to us through communion with the Creator of all reality. These gifts, which lie latent within us, will become manifest in our physical existence, leading us onward to ever greater purpose and greater possibilities. Mankind becomes enriched by our gifts because we become co-creators with the Divine whose work is not made of perishable material but of eternal reality. Human realization is therefore, unlimited.

Our evolutionary development depends upon all our efforts,

our failures, and our successes for everything we do is ultimately, soul growth. There is no such thing as failure when your heart earnestly seeks to be guided by the truths that your soul reveals to you. Even when we feel our progress is slow and laborious, it is a glorious road to follow. It is never a futile attempt to follow the path of Light that comes only through communion with the Holy One. Our individual place in our material world aids in the fruition of Spirit through our gifts, even though they may appear to be unappreciated by many. To others who recognize what we have to give, our contributions are indispensable. Living from Divine Intent, we can come into our Divine Inheritance and live with the very Essence of Life and Wisdom.

One does not need to be a rocket scientist to know that our world is headed toward some type of planetary catastrophe. Our global civilization is undergoing tremendous changes, which are affecting us physically, emotionally, and spiritually. Violence, apathy, terrorism, drug and alcohol addictions, economic upheavals, religious wars, bigotry, intolerance, abuse, nuclear weapons testing, and environmental neglect are just some of the reminders that we are living in troubled times.

Millions of people worldwide have experienced a spiritual phenomenon called a near-death experience. In the very early 1980's George Gallup Jr. conducted a poll and on the basis of that poll estimated that *8 million* people in the United States had a near-death experience. Today, it is estimated over twenty million in the U.S. alone, and similar statistics are coming in from around the world. Extensive research studies have been conducted in this field, and there is a single, unifying message to humanity that comes from the mouths of near-death experiencers and others who encountered the Light of our Creator through similar experiences. That message is **LOVE ONE ANOTHER!** There is often a sense of urgency associated with this message to humanity from these people, and they feel compelled to share that message with others. Overwhelmingly, the lives of these individuals have been transformed spiritually. As a society, this remarkable transformation in the lives of those who have encountered the Light requires us to contemplate the message that is being brought to us by these loving messengers of the Light.

In June 1981, six children saw a vision of the Virgin Mary on a mountain in Medugorje. The Virgin Mary gave the children messages to pass on to humanity. All the messages speak of peace, prayer, fasting, conversion, and confession, all of which influences a person seeking a spiritual change and union with God. Doctors and scientists rigorously tested the children using the latest, technological equipment to determine if the children's behavior was pathological. They determined that the children's visions were not pathological, but rather, a state of contemplation of connected communication with a presence only they could see and hear. Since then, more than ten million people have made the pilgrimage to Medugorje in search of spiritual and physical healings. Today, it is considered a spiritual world phenomenon.

Why are so many individuals experiencing spiritual phenomenon during this particular time in our history? Why is there a surge of global spiritual consciousness awakening and leading us back toward our Divine connections? Perhaps the answer can be found in Acts 2:17:18. *"In the last days, God said, I will pour out my Holy Spirit upon all mankind, and your sons and daughters shall prophesy, and your young men shall see visions, and your old men dream dreams. Yes, the Holy Spirit shall come upon all my servants, men and women alike, and they shall prophesy."*

I wonder if the Creator is trying by all means possible to get our attention? I wonder if all the spiritual visions that ordinary people are having is something that we should pay attention to as that Bible passage suggests? If so, we can't afford to turn our eyes and ears away from the One who seems to be revealing to us that we must consciously begin to purify our individual lives so that we may become channels for the Light to bring love into the world.

I believe the message is very clear for all of us. If humanity is to evolve, it is imperative that we take individual responsibility to prepare ourselves for a future of hope. If we continue to live from our ego attachment to self and materialism, we will fail to awaken our destiny as set by our Creator. But as we begin to open a pathway to our consciousness that reflects our commitment to live from our spiritual nature, we will be led into a new condition of life. We need only *ask* for Divine assistance if we are unsure how to initiate a transformation. We will receive that help.

The only effectual way to discern Divine Will is to align one's will to Divine Will. When Supreme Intelligence guides our soul, we will always choose good over evil for the limitless bounty of Divine Wisdom is the condition in which true happiness exists. When we do this, then we will know that we have been called to live a Divine life. When we hear His Voice within, then we can be assured that we will rest in a place of tranquility, as our whole being becomes a life that brings blessings to others. The Light in our soul will reveal to others that there is a steadfast faith and assurance in the One who has called us to live a transformed life. All power will be given to us to live our fullest potential as children of the Light.

In our finite mind, we can never imagine our Divine Inheritance that will be given to us when we become transformed in Spirit. When we respond to our individual calling, we will become wrought by the Holy tenderness of Divine Love. If our souls are functioning freely through our physical bodies, we will know the limitless bounty of the Divine Life force to sustain the calling of our earthly mission. As a radiant soul shining through our physical bodies, we then enter into the fullness and the very life on earth well prepared to reveal the manifestation of Spirit in an instrument capable of voicing its reality.

Dear friend, remember this. The ego has a very limited perception of self and keeps reiterating falsehoods and half-truths in order to seek gratification on a lower plane of being. Your soul is in touch with the very essence of Creation, and it knows what your potential is. Spirit's Voice within knows that when you listen to it instead of ego's voice, your difficulties will cease. So, make use of the tools that Spirit has given you so you can develop into a masterpiece in accordance with Divine Purpose.

CHAPTER 15

FROM MY HEART TO YOURS

When love dwells within the heart, the Holy temple of one's soul opens and enjoys sweet communion with the Divine.

I am but a small grain of sand in the palm of your hand God, and yet you called me to communicate your message of love and hope to the world. I promised that I would serve you above all, no matter what you asked of me, and no matter what obstacles I would have to bear. Thank you for helping me with this "calling" and for giving me the intimate personal knowledge that you are always helping me. Without that, I could not, and would not be able to carry out the promise I made to you on that miraculous day, January 29, 1979. Thank you for letting me experience how deep your unconditional love is for **all of us**. In your eyes, each and every one of us **without exception** is a precious diamond. Each facet of every diamond is being shaped and polished by your Loving Hands with your Love that dwells within us.

Each day is a miracle that you give us. We have the opportunity to share your Love with others. Reaching down in our hearts allows us to experience the depth of a Love so deep and abiding, that it is incomprehensible by man's limited awareness. This is your Love God, indwelling within us. You are within us regardless that some may not call you "God." You transcend words

and imagery, but you are revealed to us as Love. When we are
in touch with your Love, not only does it nourish our physical,
mental, and spiritual selves, it also serves to reach outside us as
an extension of you and ourselves to our fellow man.

We are blessed beyond measure when we become vessels
filled to overflowing with your Love, which cannot be contained
and never ceases to pour itself into our infiniteness. We are truly
one with you and as such, are more than we can possibly begin
to imagine. This is why we yearn for your indwelling Holy Spirit
to teach us more about you and your precious Love.

Prepare the way ahead, and we shall follow you by faith. We
shall become as trusting as small children, holding tightly onto
your hand and following where you lead. We do not know the
path you will lead us nor what lies ahead, but we will follow your
lead. Your ways are perfect. Your ways are meant for our highest
good. Your ways are truthful and loving. Your promise to us, *"I
will be with you always, to the end of the age"* (Matthew 28:20)
assures us that you are with us even though at times, we think
you are not.

Assuring us that you are always with us, strengthens our
inner being to trust sometimes without seeing or hearing. Our
intuitive nature is the soul's voice within that seeks to guide
us in all things and in all ways toward the realization of God-
consciousness within. You are the still small Voice that lovingly
speaks to us and guides us in ways that nourishes our higher self.

Your Voice within is soft, gentle, and tender. It beckons us
to walk closer to you in all of our daily activities, whether we are
alone or relating to others in some way. Your Voice within speaks
to us through the language of love and encourages us to react in
all circumstances in loving ways. When we respond accordingly,
we are blessed within with indwelling peace and unspeakable joy.
Your Love is the only thing that is everlasting and perfect. As we
express love inwardly and outwardly, that love is reflected back

to us a hundred fold, a million fold, indeed, without measure,

A loving heart knows that the expression of this love out-wardly is a freedom to explore the universe like a bird that takes to the air. Soaring from us, it is the motion that sustains the energy of that love. We need only be reminded that when we are fearful of expressing our love, that only in releasing it are we truly free from our fears and our limitations. Love is truly the key to the universe. There are no locks to unlock within the universe. The door for you is always open through a loving heart.

You have taught us, *"Ask, and it shall be given you; seek, and* ye shall find; knock and the door shall be opened unto you." (Mat-thew 7:7) You call us before you because we are your children, and you love us unceasingly. You will never force us to come to you, but oh, how happy you are when we return to the aware-ness of who we are in relationship to you. Why, the heavens must abound with song and dance, and the choirs of angels must be rejoicing and singing whenever this happens. Truly, we are never the same once that awareness comes to us. We enter into a state of communion with you that no force can tear apart except our own individual choice to do so.

And yet, your choice to love us unconditionally without strings attached, endures beyond time, space, and eternity. You will always love us no matter what! Thank you for that kind of unconditional love. It allows us to recognize our errors, make amends and begin anew. We will always be grateful for new beginnings in you and in knowing you are always beside us ready to pick us up when we fall. Many of us can only conceive of a limited form of your Love. If we have not experienced your Love directly and personally, we cannot comprehend through our imagination what your Love is like. Because we seek to know thee more intimately, we ask that you participate fully in our lives when we dare to risk expressing our love outwardly toward others.

We will hold onto your hand tightly as we risk opening up ourselves to your Love so that we may be your reflection to the world. As we do this, we will feel your deeply rooted Love welling up inside until it bursts forward from us like a dam without restraint until it majestically cascades over someone in need.

My prayer for humanity is that one by one, each individual will raise his or her consciousness to your Loving Light so that you can begin a make-over with that person as you did with me. As they begin their journey toward a higher spiritual consciousness, carry them when they tire, encourage them when they stumble, and love them eternally. By your Divine Grace, humanity can develop spiritually on an evolutionary thrust to merge into oneness with your Light of Love. Then humanity can in unison, sing the glorious song of thanksgiving: *"Amazing grace, how sweet the sound, that saved a wretch like me. I once was lost, but now I'm found, was blind, but now I see."*

CHAPTER 16

THE IMPORTANT MESSAGE

The eye is not the only way of seeing;
the ear is not the only way of hearing.

One day during my prayerful communion with my Great Comforter, I was led to a passage in the Bible that characterizes my faith and your faith in the Beloved. Jesus said, *"Because thou has seen me, thou has believed: but blessed are they that have not seen and ye have believed."* (John 20:29) This is my favorite passage in the Bible because when people get all caught up in admiring my personal encounter with the Light of God, I think how glorious other people's faith is when they have not seen and have not heard. I admire others for this reason more than others should admire me!

Keeping that faith and not letting it go will assure you that you are being molded into a masterpiece resembling the Divine. Your spiritual equilibrium will manifest in ways that are uniquely meant for you, given to you by Divine Grace. That is the way true spirituality is meant to be. You are not a duplicate copy of anyone else so why should your personal spiritual journey through this life duplicate someone else's journey? There is no one in this entire universe that is just like you! Your individuality is that which God has given to you alone. Your spirituality is also uniquely your own.

Cherish and cultivate your own path toward growing into a fully mature child of God through an enhanced awareness of God's personal Life within you, expressed through you as Divine Love. I can promise you that you will begin to view life and people differently, and you will become more loving, compassionate, and peaceful. When love resides within your heart and soul, Spirit can talk with you and speak to your soul in such a gentle, tender way that you will begin to see things as Spirit does. No longer will you seek attachment to unhealthy relationships or neurotic needs, but you will be able to radiate a spirit of joy deep within your soul that liberates you and gives clarity and meaning to your existence. At the end of our journey through this life, we will awaken to a new life with our Creator, and we will experience the ineffable eternal ecstasy of Spirit's Loving Presence. When you have your life review, you will clearly understand the purpose of your earthly life, and you will determine if you applied that knowledge well.

If you learned anything from what I have shared with you so far, please remember this - *You must learn to see yourself not as others see you or even through your narrow vision determined by your ego, but rather with the vision of your true self, your soul, that part of the Divine Presence within you.* Your physical body governed by your ego will be cast aside at the moment of death, but your spiritual soul continues to live on eternally. Earthly life has been given as a gift to you to **learn to love**. Right now your soul is primarily concerned that you live your life being a good person who avoids harming yourself or another by thought, word, or deed.

To prepare you for reading the final pages in this book, I feel compelled to share the wisdom of a dream I had. I shared the content of my dream with a friend the day after my dream. He documented it as part of a research study he was conducting for his Ph.D. dissertation. At that time, I had absolutely no idea the dream would be prophetic and related to this book.

In my dream, I was standing on marble steps looking out at thousands of people mingling with one another. My hands were outstretched upward toward God when God began to speak to me concerning an important message He was going to bring to the people through me. The problem, however, was that others would not believe that God was revealing Himself to me, a common woman. So in order to help raise the consciousness of the people, God was going to give me small, sample messages to share with them. When the people saw that those messages came true, they would be more apt to trust and be receptive when God brought the important message through me.

The first small message involved a bride who was about to be married. She was standing beside a large oak tree in front of a huge mansion. The photographer was taking her photo just minutes before she was going to be married. Suddenly, a vision appeared in my mind. The bride was going to announce that she was going to cancel the wedding. After I had that vision in my mind, I proceeded to tell the huge crowd of people that the bride was going to announce her wedding cancellation. The crowd became very angry with me because the bride was only moments away from being married, and they felt I had no right to say she was going to cancel her wedding. Soon however, the bride announced she was canceling her wedding. The crowd responded with dismay and then turned to me and shouted, "How did you know this information?" I replied, "The message came to me from God. God wants to show you that you can learn to trust that the message is coming from God through me."

Receiving a second message from God moments later, I turned to the crowd and said, "There's a swimming pool over there. In it you will find three men at the bottom of the pool." The crowd glanced over and exclaimed, "We don't see anyone." I answered, "Dive in and rescue them." Hesitating at first, some people entered the water and brought three men up to the surface and revived them. "What you said was true," someone said.

"How did you know there were three men at the bottom of the pool?"

Once again I announced, "It was a message from God coming through me. God is the Source of my knowledge, and God is using these examples to show you that what I am telling you can be trusted with accuracy. God wants your faith to be elevated so that when He is ready to bring His important message to you, you will believe." My dream ended before the big important message from God came.

I didn't think about that dream until the final pages of this book were written. I woke up suddenly at 3:00 a.m. one morning. Normally, I do not wake up at 3:00 a.m. much less begin any kind of activity in the middle of the night. But I felt "led" to pick up my pen and notebook and resume working on this book. I was very awake, refreshed, and alert. This was unusual because normally I am just the opposite if I happen to wake up at 3:00 a.m. But I also knew that when I felt so alert when I was suddenly awakened in the middle of the night that I was being led by Spirit to work on this book. So I walked to the living room and turned the stereo on softly so I wouldn't wake my family, and I began to work on the inspired writing for this book.

What followed was something I had not anticipated or planned at all! During the course of my writing, I was reminded to let the words flow onto the paper and not to question what was appearing on my paper. The writing that appeared on my paper was the "**important message from God**" brought through me as prophesied during my dream.

I completely understood after reading the message from God that my dream was prophetic after all, and relevant to the contents of this book. I had often wondered why the writing of this book was taking on such an intimate disclosure of my life since I am a very private woman, but now I understood. Like my prophetic dream, people would have to know me intimately in order to elevate their faith for acceptance of God's message that was going to be brought through me. My life and all of my experiences are as illustrated in my dream, small sample messages to show you that there *is* a Spiritual Presence working within and through me. The readers of this book are like the crowd of people in my dream who first need to be shown that God is indeed, making His Voice heard throughout my life and that the Voice can be trusted.

My entire life cannot easily be dismissed simply as a series of coincidences, or the result of a mentally unstable woman. I am psychologically healthy. I function quite well in society and live a very fulfilling and beautiful life. Mental illness has the opposite effect upon an individual. One is not capable of functioning well, and often times, it interferes with one's life to such a degree that life takes on no meaning or purpose. Mental processes become confusing to the extent that one often times is not capable of holding a job. Relationships become difficult to handle. In essence, mental illness disrupts a person's life, while my own life has been enhanced by everything that has occurred.

While it may be true that my life experiences may sound too ominous to be believed, think about gravity for a moment. Imagine looking at the planet earth from thousands of miles in outer space. You can see the continents, the mighty oceans, and what appears to be a perfectly rimmed circle of our planet. Why doesn't the water from the ocean at the bottom of our planet fall in a downward path toward outer space? The answer of course is gravity. Can you see gravity? Can you touch it, smell it, or hear it or taste it? With my human senses I cannot and neither can you. Yet, I can accept with complete trust that many physicists have calculated the effects of gravity and understand the tremendous force or pressure being exerted upon our planet to keep the oceans in their place. That thought boggles my mind! Can you see, smell, taste, hear or touch the wind? I can't. I can only experience the **effects** of the wind. I have learned to accept its reality without relying on any of my physical senses to prove its authenticity.

I cannot comprehend in my limited awareness how I spoke with my mother who lived five-hundred miles away and heard her sweet voice as I was standing in my kitchen holding a telephone to my ear. Any electrical engineer can explain the mechanics to me, but when I look outdoors at the wires stretching from pole to pole or if I take the telephone apart and observe the small chips inside, I am still left bewildered. We take those things for granted because we have seen their **results** affect our lives in some way. Thus, we accept and rely upon many things we don't understand. So it is with the mysterious realm of the Spirit. Spiritual life is not governed by the physical five senses. Yet its reality can also be accepted by the results the spiritual effects have upon our lives. We can learn to **trust** the unseen world through the same manner as our limited understanding of the physical world, and that is through **faith**.

I can promise you that nothing in this book has been fabricated. Everything stated is an accurate description of my journey through this life and my union with God. I have no wish to stroke my ego for what I have experienced nor for my service to humanity. My only desire has been to fulfill my promise I made to the Light of God that beautiful day in 1979. I will continue to love God for eternity, and I will continue to speak of God's unconditional love for **all of us** until I draw my final breath.

Now I completely understand your reluctance to believe that what I am espousing may be considered delusional or fanatical, especially when you are being told to trust me in this way. But please believe me, I am a very sane individual. When I had my near-death-like experience and encounter with the Light, I was shown during my life preview the kind of cynicism and disbelief I would encounter when I told others what my Great Teacher revealed to me. But I promised the Light of God that I would accept this calling no matter what I had to endure. It would be

my gift of service to the One who graced me with this miraculous encounter, and who transformed my life forever. Ultimately,
you will have to choose between your ego's need to disbelieve
everything I am sharing with you, or to trust by your faith in
the One who loves you beyond comprehension that what I am
sharing with you is the simple truth. Your choice!

Dear friend, as you read the following message that appeared
spontaneously during my inspired writing session with God at
3:00 o'clock in the morning, may God's Holy Wisdom speak
lovingly to your heart and may your soul cherish its truth.

CHAPTER 17

HEAR HIS VOICE

Withdraw now from the senses of the material world and come into the infinite and eternal garden of the Spirit. The Holy One awaits!

"My dear sweet children,

My Love is for all who welcome it. Those who choose not to recognize my Love will be separated from me by their own choice. I will never cause separation from my children and myself, **never!** Separation from me is caused by the ego which assumes that my Love chooses worthy children and casts aside unworthy children. Never believe this! You are perfect in my image when you reside in my Love. The core of your being is my Divinity given to you without strings attached. I reside within you, whether you are aware of me or not.

All too often, mankind's language, symbolism and the various interpretations of my Love have confused my children to the extent that I have become so different to so many of my children. I am falsely accused of being a God who loves some and despises others. Never accept this as your truth. Whatever despicable act you have done, I can forgive you. You have been made whole again in my image the moment you choose to draw near to me in my Love.

To all who judge others unworthy of my Love, I speak to you and say, **all** are worthy of my Love. You must not cause separation from my Love by judging others. My Love is all-inclusive and will never be used as a measure of one's worth to me. It is sad to see my children argue and alienate one from another simply because of their differences. When you can see others as I see you, you will heal the discord among you, and you will begin to unfold my Divine Purpose in your lives. That condition occurs when the ego has been transformed.

Remember my words, *"Love one another, just as I love you."* Accept one another as your brother and sister and love them as your very own. Resist the urge to use me as your weapon of scorn toward others. You will always find peace within you when you are willing to replace conditional love with my Love.

A time is coming when my Love will rule, but in order for that to happen, my children must take personal responsibility to allow my Divine Love and Spirit to awaken within your sleeping hearts. Like a whisper in your ear, I am reminding you that my Divine Presence is within you. Pay attention to the times when I speak to you, urging you to make loving choices in your life. The more loving you become, the more you will recognize my Presence within you.

Radiating my unconditional Love from you will teach others what real love is, and that love will begin to multiply throughout the lands. Think not of love as an emotion, but rather as my power to change the course of mankind. There is a day coming when my children will live together with my Love in their hearts. It will be a time of great joy and peace. But first, my children must learn about unconditional love and then make loving choices in their lives. Those choices will be my power manifesting to bring about the new beginning I have planned for you.

My dear sweet children, you are worthy of my Love. Do not allow cynicism to lead you away from what I am telling you. Cast aside your intolerances and differences. Cherish one another as I cherish you.

Your loving Heavenly Creator"

COMMENT

Immediately following the message that appeared on my paper, I went to my Bible and prayerfully asked God to lead me to a passage to verify that the message that came through was authentic as coming from God. With the Bible closed and held over my heart, I closed my eyes and began to move my right index finger about two inches above the closed pages. While I was doing that, I was talking to God so tenderly, filling myself up with so much love for the One who loves **all of us as if we were the only one on the face of the earth.** Receptive to the Spirit within, I asked this question. "God, you promised me the day you called me to yourself that you would help me to bring your message of love and hope to humanity. I want to be absolutely certain that the message that came through on my writing paper is actually coming from you and that it is truthful in its content. I want to be sure this message fulfills your promise to bring your Love and hope for the future. This message will be read by many people. Can they be assured that it is indeed, your message of love and hope for their spiritual lives?" With my eyes still closed and still moving my index finger back and forth, I waited until I saw a flash of white light in the corner of my left eye. Then I poked my finger into the closed pages, opened the Bible where my index finger had poked into and began reading the passages. This is what appeared:

Hebrews 6:17-19

"When we make a vow, we use the name of someone greater than ourselves, and the vow settles all arguments. To those who were to receive what he promised, God wanted to make it very clear that he would never change his purpose; so he added his vow to the promise. There are these two things, then, that cannot change and about which God cannot lie. So we who have found safety with him are greatly encouraged to hold firmly to the hope placed before us. We have this hope as an anchor for our lives. It is safe and sure, and goes through the curtain of the heavenly temple into the inner sanctuary."

A FINAL THOUGHT

It has been a great privilege to serve my Great Teacher by completing this book that I was instructed to write during my near-death-like experience in 1979. I do not know when my service will be through, but one thing I am certain; I will always remain an open vessel for the Light, ready to serve in any way I am called. Actually, this journey through life is about receiving the ability to hear His Voice so we can learn and be who we truly are.

Each passing day will bring us closer to our homeward destination, so it's very important that we apply that knowledge in all aspects of our lives from this day forward. We can never change what happened yesterday, so rather than focusing our energy on past events, or fear, guilt, blame, etc., it is far better to focus on today and the love we can give to ourselves and others. Today is the only day we can choose to respond from a new perception of the true loving person we are.

Listen to your soul's voice within that whispers your name, reminding you to respond to the small as well as the large gestures of kindness and compassion in thought, word, or deed. As long as you respond from the indwelling energy of Divine Love that you are, you will fulfill your soul's purpose here on earth, and you will not have lived in vain.

You have perhaps read many books on the subject of spirituality. I have given you some words to contemplate in this book.

Many religious people talked about God for centuries, and still, our daily lives seem strewn with discord. Talk is cheap they say, and it is not by words but rather, the conscious awareness of the Presence of God within us that is the real secret to a peaceful existence.

Always remember these important truths I learned during my mystical experience and what the Light of God wanted me to promulgate to the human family.

- The Light of God lives within us.
- God wants a personal **relationship** with us.
- God is a **loving** , not a punishing God.
- God wants us to hear His Voice when He speaks to us.
- God works in us that which God would have us do.
- God manifests Himself through us to others.
- God wants us to *"love others as I love you."*

If I have played a small role in lifting your heart closer to God in some small way, then my joyous service to the Light of God has been realized. Thank you dear reader for allowing your heart to respond to the written words between the lines of this book and for taking the time to reflect upon the deeper meaning that surfaced within your heart. If you did that, and it stirred up loving responses and brought you inner peace, then you have heard His Voice. May your own mystical life blossom in the understanding that your Great Teacher dwells unceasingly in your soul, nurturing and guiding you in all things and keeps you eternally in His Precious Love.

LISTEN CLOSELY, AND HEAR HIS VOICE!

ABOUT THE AUTHOR

Nancy Clark graduated from Women's Medical College at the University of Pennsylvania specializing in Cytology, the study of cells. For thirty years she worked in the research and clinical Cytology arena at a major university and other laboratories studying cells for the early detection of cancer and diseases. This scientific background enabled her to analyze her own transcendent experiences objectively before arriving at the ultimate conclusion that parallel realities do indeed, exist. Now retired, she is passionately devoting her life to the spiritual work that is so important to her by inspiring others toward the Transcendent nature of life and into the mysterious union with the Light of God.

She is a member of the National League of American Penwomen, International Association Near-Death Studies, Inc. (IANDS), and the Academy of Spirituality and Paranormal Studies, Inc. She is the founder and president of the Columbus, Ohio IANDS organization since 1984. Nancy Clark has a public speaking background and has given talks for colleges, universities, professional conferences, churches, hospitals, community organizations as well as being interviewed on radio and television, and acted as a consultant on near-death experiences for the media.

Nancy appreciates your comments and personally answers all emails. Contact her at **nancyclarkauthor@gmail.com**. For more information about Nancy Clark, please go to her website at: **www.freewebs.com/nancy-clark**

CPSIA information can be obtained at www.ICGtesting.com
Printed in the USA
BVOW040416190613

323712BV00001B/161/P